STRONG FOUNDATIONS

DRIFFIELD'S AERODROME FROM 1917 TO 2OOO

by

Geoff Simmons
and
Barry Abraham

HUTTON PRESS
2001

Published by

The Hutton Press Ltd.,
130 Canada Drive, Cherry Burton,
Beverley, East Yorkshire HU17 7SB

Copyright © 2001
Geoff Simmons & Barry Abraham

Printed and bound by
The College Press
a division of the University of Hull

ISBN 1 902709 13 6

DEDICATION:

We must not forget all those who served at Driffield, the casualties of the bombing
and those who did not return from operations.

Our wives, Audrey and Penny who not only have endured our interest and work
in aviation but gave support and kept spirits high during the compilation of "Strong Foundations".

CONTENTS

The Zeppelin Outrages.

Now that the ban has been removed respecting the publication of news of raids made by Zepps., it may be of interest to recall the fact that Driffield was the first Yorkshire town to have bombs dropped by these murderous machines. The visit was made on the night of Friday, June 4th, 1915, when the machine was seen somewhere in the neighbourhood of the Parish Church about 11 p.m. It was ascertained that it had entered by way of Bridlington, and after reaching Driffield seemed to be in doubt as to its whereabouts. It then cruised round by Langtoft and Sledmere, eventually passing over Driffield on its way home about 1 a.m. on the Saturday morning. Two bombs were dropped, which caused great explosions, startling many of the inhabitants in the town and district from their slumbers. The first bomb was dropped in the garden behind Springfield House, in Eastgate South, doing considerable damage to the root crops and surrounding trees. The houses in the neighbourhood were also much shaken, and some hundreds of squares of glass were broken, while pieces of shrapnel were picked up at great distances from the scene of explosion, and many people received cuts from broken glass. There was only an interval of a few minutes between the explosions, the second bomb falling in a field in Meadow Lane, belonging to Mr. Walmsley, opposite the first gate house, where it made a large cavity, very much resembling a pond, but no other damage was done.

Rumours spread, which were greatly exaggerated, and the town was visited by thousands of people on the Saturday and Sunday, many coming from Hull, who expressed their astonishment at so slight a damage.

Many people had the impression that this visit was one of searching out for a good landing, and this would appear to be correct, for on the following Sunday night another Zeppelin come over Bridlington and Driffield and found its way to Hull, doing a good deal of damage.

This brought the lighting restrictions more strongly into force, and special constables were enrolled to do duty on "Air raid warning" nights, and although we have had many warnings and Zeppelins passing over the town, which caused the inhabitants much worry and anxiety, we have been very fortunate that no further bombs were dropped in Driffield, after seeing what other towns have experienced.

Driffield Times and General Advertiser report on the bombing of Driffield.

Zeppelins and an aerodrome was opened at Copmanthorpe.
The BE 2c, generally, allocated to the Home Defence Squadrons for interceptor duties. This particular machine built by Blackburn at their Leeds Olympia Works has had the machine's serial number blacked out by the censor.

(JMB/GSL Collection)

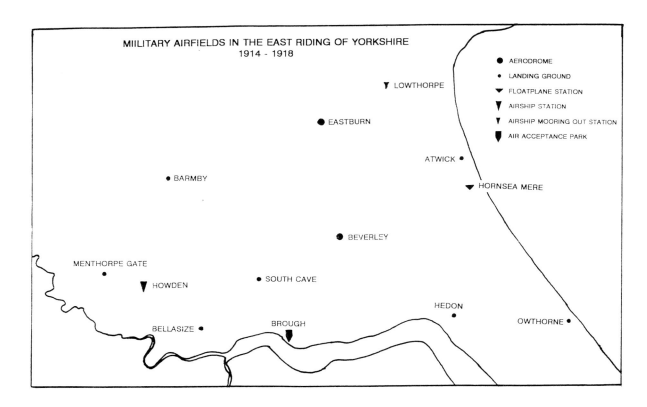

MIILITARY AIRFIELDS IN THE EAST RIDING OF YORKSHIRE
1914 - 1918

● AERODROME
• LANDING GROUND
▼ FLOATPLANE STATION
▼ AIRSHIP STATION
▼ AIRSHIP MOORING OUT STATION
▼ AIR ACCEPTANCE PARK

▼ LOWTHORPE

● EASTBURN

ATWICK •

▼ HORNSEA MERE

• BARMBY

● BEVERLEY

MENTHORPE GATE
•

▼ HOWDEN

• SOUTH CAVE

HEDON
•

OWTHORNE •

BELLASIZE •

BROUGH ▼

Aerodromes and landing grounds established for the Home Defence Squadrons of the Royal Flying Corps in the East Riding of Yorkshire.

Armstrong Whitworth F.K.3, 5510, on the establishment of No.47 Squadron when based at RFC Beverley during 1916.
(JMB/GSL Collection)

12

A Squadron comprised a Headquarters Flight plus "A", "B", and "C" Flights distributed over three or four aerodromes, for instance No. 33 Squadron RFC was based at Beverley, Bramham Moor (Tadcaster), Coal Aston and Doncaster, with landing grounds requisitioned in the surrounding districts. "C" Flight of No. 33 shared Beverley with No. 47 Squadron which had formed there when it opened in March 1916.

The standard aeroplane of the Royal Flying Corps Home Defence squadrons was the B.E. 2c, a two seat tractor biplane powered by a Royal Aircraft Factory 70h.p. air cooled in-line engine. Developed by the Royal Aircraft Factory at Farnborough and in common with many aeroplanes of that period production was sub-contracted to many manufacturers. Although a two seater the majority of Home Defence sorties were flown solo. The offensive armament was a fixed Vickers machine-gun and various bombs, grapnels and explosive darts were carried to pierce the Zeppelin envelope in the hope that the gas would escape and could then be ignited by incendiary bullets. This was to be accomplished from above the Zeppelin.

Defence policy at the time was to have two aeroplanes at readiness and one on standby. The procedure was for one to take off as soon as a warning was received and patrol over the aerodrome at 8 -10,000ft for two hours, this required adequate warning time to allow for climb to patrol height, the second aeroplane to follow 90 minutes later. A system of signals on the ground was developed to indicate the latest known direction of the intruder. Often the readiness aeroplanes would be detached to an adjacent landing ground, a rudimentary place little more than a meadow with shelter for ground staff.

By 1917 the Zeppelin threat was considered to be lower and as the attrition rate to pilots on the Western Front was growing to such an extent an increase in pilot training was seen to be required. As a result the number of aeroplanes required for the Home Defence commitment of the U.K. based squadrons was scaled down. No. 47 Squadron had left Beverley for Salonika in September 1916, and No. 33 Squadron moved into Lincolnshire in October 1916 for the defence of south Yorkshire. Beverley then reverted to a training establishment, but it still retained its listing as a Home Defence landing ground. The Home Defence responsibilities for North Yorkshire were then with No. 76 Squadron based on Ripon, Copmanthorpe, Helperby and Catterick from 1916 to the end of the war.

In the early days of the war some ab-initio pilot training was carried out at civil flying schools or at a few Reserve Aeroplane Squadrons to a limited solo proficiency. The pupil then progressed to military flying training at Netheravon. Following being trained to be an officer and gentleman and a more accomplished pilot, he was sent on to a squadron where his advanced training continued in the hands of his senior pilots. The number of Reserve Aeroplane Schools was increased to meet the demand for pilots and they were renamed Reserve Squadrons on the 13th of January 1916. Training standards were constantly under review and in March 1916 Qualification Tests were drawn up as follows :-

1)	The Pilot must have spent at least 15 hours in the air solo.
2)	He must have flown a service aeroplane satisfactorily.
3)	He must have carried out a cross country flight of at least 60 miles successfully. During this flight he must land at two outside landing places under the supervision of an officer of the RFC.
4)	He will climb to 6,000 ft and remain at that height for at least 15 minutes, after which he will land with his engine stopped, the aeroplane first touching the ground within a circular mark of 50 yards diameter. This test can be combined with (3) if proper supervision can be arranged.
5)	He will make two landings in the dark assisted by flares.

During late 1916 it was decided to categorise the Reserve Squadrons into Elementary and Higher types, students moved from one to another before posting to a service squadron. This reduced the training commitment on units working up to operational status. The test requirements for graduate pilots were constantly under review and by 1918 had been revised for the various categories of front line pilots being trained for duty in the newly formed Royal Air Force. The training establishments went through several changes of title, i.e Training Squadron, Training Depot Station, although the training function did not change with the alteration of name.

In mid 1916 the Military authorities requisitioned one hundred and eighty acres from Eastburn Farm and a further sixty from Kelleythorpe Farm located two miles to the South-West of Great Driffield and construction work commenced in December 1916 on the technical site to provide the facilities for the shelter and engineering support of the aeroplanes, plus the classrooms for ground training and the regimental site providing domestic accommodation for the permanent staff and pilots in training. In common with the construction of other aerodromes at this period the building work at Eastburn was carried out by civilian contractors. The raw materials, in what was standard practice at this time, were brought into the area by

The SE 5a was the advanced training machine at RFC Eastburn/RAF Driffield where 36 were listed on the establishment of No 21 TDS.

(G. Phillips via MGS Collection)

Crashes were frequent at the training establishments, although not often as severe as when this Spad 7 hit an aeroplane shed roof and crashed at RAF Driffield on the 11th of November 1919.

(G. Phillips via MGS Collection)

SE 5a, D3433 "A", inverted on the flying field of 21 TDS.

(JMB/GSL Collection)

The Aeroplane Repair Shed was of similar construction but with only one roof truss span, giving an internal width of 100ft and the same number of bays as the coupled sheds, two external annexe Plane Stores, 58ft by 34ft, were built on one side. Unlike the aeroplane sheds the ARS was closed at each end by six corrugated metal sliding doors. Unfortunately the end supports for the doors are not apparent from contemporary photographs, but it is reasonable to assume that they were built as double piers of brick.

The aeroplane establishment of aeroplanes at No. 21 TS as listed in the Survey is given as 36 S.E.5 and, the standard training aeroplane of the period, 36 Avro 504. The collection of contemporary photographs also shows various aeroplanes at Eastburn/Driffield including Spad 7, Sopwith Snipe, Airco D.H. 5, Avro 504K and an interior photograph of the Aeroplane Repair Shed shows a considerable number of S.E. 5a machines, stored without the upper and lower mainplanes. This collection reveals that crash landings were not unusual as there are photographs of S.E. 5a's in various states of damage.

An oblique photograph from the air shows that to the east of the aeroplane sheds along the road side towards Driffield there were five Bessoneau Hangars. These were transportable timber and canvas hangars of French design, the standard unit in use by the RFC/RAF, a Type H, measured approximately 64ft wide and the Eastburn examples appear to have been the 74ft long versions. These are not included in the Survey but are thought to have been erected to provide facilities during the building construction stage, and afterwards retained on site.

Correspondence from Wg Cdr W.E. Dunn OBE (RAF Rtd.), dated 1982/1983, recalls that before joining the RAF as a regular in November 1918 he visited the aerodrome at Kelleythorpe on most weekends where alongside the road to Market Weighton was a line of Bessoneau hangars that were being used to store the salvaged remains of crashed aeroplanes and from a friendly Sergeant he was able to augment his collection of souvenirs from aircraft.

The administrative and domestic quarters occupied 25 acres to the south of the road. The buildings, other than the Aeroplane Sheds, and including the huts on the Technical site existing at the time would be the standard military wooden huts supported on brick piers. Domestic drainage and sewage was piped to settling tanks to the south-east of the Regimental buildings and adjacent to one of the tributaries to the Driffield Trout Stream, a practice that would not be approved of today.

All the planned buildings were completed by February 1919 but the personnel numbers were not achieved prior to closure. At this time Eastburn was renamed RAF Driffield to avoid confusion with the RAF aerodrome at Eastbourne in Sussex.

The wartime expansion in training was accomplished by opening two new training schools and the creation of twenty Reserve (training) squadrons in Canada, the precursor to the Empire Air Training Scheme of the Second World War. During 1917 the nucleus of these squadrons were formed in north-eastern Britain prior to their embarkation for Canada. The training of Empire airmen continued at RAF training schools and on the 1st of March 1919 Lt W.R. Reid, an 18 year old Canadian, took off from Eastburn climbed above the aerodrome and for some unknown reason went into a spin, crashed back onto the flying field and was killed. He was given a full military burial in Driffield Cemetery.

No. 202 Squadron, ex No. 2 (Naval) Squadron, arrived from Belgium, via Dover on the 27th of March 1919 as a cadre having relinquished their Airco D.H. 9 aeroplanes and they stayed to December prior to moving to Spittlegate and disbandment in January 1920. Also joining them at Driffield two days later, by the same route from the Continent, No. 217 Squadron (ex No. 17 (Naval) Sqn), arrived as a cadre, i.e in accordance with standard practice at the time comprised 2 officers, 1 SNCO and 12 other ranks and stayed to disbandment on the 19th of October 1919 and demobilisation.

The first year of peace allowed the home based military units to settle into a more relaxed routine and on the 6th of June 1919 RAF Driffield held a sports day under the auspices of the Commanding Officer Major Murray DSO., DFC, when apart from the usual races etc. other events were held such as Tilting the Bucket, Mop Fights and, for the WRAF, an Apple Race in which they had to run 50 yards retrieve an apple by mouth from a bucket of water and run back. An Officers versus Men, Tug of War was won by the Men. Prizes, donated by the staff of The Driffield Steam Laundry Company, were presented by the C.O.'s wife. During the afternoon the spectators were entertained by the Driffield Town Band.

The low flying exploits of Captain Balfour seem to have set a precedent for certain pilots at RAF Driffield. There is a report of some pilots flying through Driffield town railway station where the distance between escaped with a severe shaking but the pilot sustained some injuries which meant hospitalisation. Two Virginias of No. 58 had been in formation and flew past the light house when one of them was heard to have engines misfiring, it turned round and forced landed striking a sheep which was killed. The other aircraft landed alongside to help and took off a little later. The Virginia which crashed was serialled J7422 and a write off.

Ron Southgate who had trained at art school joined the RAF at Uxbridge and was posted to Driffield as an Aircraftman in September 1936. He had lived at Selby so it was like coming home. Recalling the Vickers Virginias, his only contact with them was to help tie them down during windy conditions because the hangars were not yet ready to hold them. Working in the Sergeants Mess, he soon put on weight through generous portions of food so moved on to a new job on the station doing wood carving, thereby exploiting his artistic talents. He did a crucifix for the station chapel along with pencil portraits selling them a 2/6d each! After leaving Driffield, he went to Cardington for training in Balloon operations then teaching WAAFs who were still civilians at the beginning of the Second World War, for the next four years being demobbed as a Corporal.

On 26th October, the AOC No. 3 (B) Group, Air Vice-Marshall P. H. L. Playfair CB CVO MC carried out an inspection of the squadrons and base.

Driffield had some surprise visitors at the beginning of January 1937! No. 97 (B) Squadron which was based at Boscombe Down aerodrome near Salisbury in Wiltshire was transferring to its new base at Leconfield - the first squadron to be based at this new aerodrome which had just opened. It was flying Handley Page Heyford bombers but could not land at Leconfield because of the sodden state of the grass landing area, diverting to Driffield the 24 airmen in the machines landed after the 1 hour 40 minute flight from Boscombe.

No. 58 was notified of a partial re-equipment by fourteen Avro Anson I in February 1937, the first aircraft was collected from A.V. Roe & Co. Ltd at Woodford, Cheshire on 10th February but most were collected on the 11th with the last by 24th February. These aircraft were painted silver with the squadron number and individual aircraft letter painted on either side of the roundel and gave the crews experience in handling modern aircraft, although the Virginias were still retained. No. 215 got their notification on 27th February 1937 that they would also have a partial re-equipment with Avro Ansons, the last aircraft being received on 24th March 1937. One of their Ansons had dual controls, however in common with Ansons supplied to other Bomber Command squadrons, not all had turrets installed, probably because production of turrets had been outpaced by manufacture of aircraft! The Anson later became the backbone aircraft of Coastal Command until the Lockheed Hudson took over and then the type made a considerable contribution in the training role of the RAF.

Two new squadrons were to be formed at Driffield, one each from Nos 58 and 215. On the 15th March 1937, No. 51(B) Sqn was re-formed at Driffield from "B" Flt of No. 58 Sqn with Virginia X under the command of F/Lt G.P. Marvin and "B" Flight of No. 215 became 75 (B) Sqn, No. 215 then operated on a two flight basis - seven Ansons and four Virginias on strength. No. 75 (B) Sqn commenced to reform at Driffield on 15th March 1937, some 47 NCOs and airmen were posted from No. 215 to No. 75 with three new pilots. The squadron had four Virginia X and seven Anson I, two of which were taken over from those allotted to No. 215. The following month Anson K6322 undershot on landing at Driffield and hit trees.

On the 24th of March, No. 58 and the new No. 51 moved to Boscombe Down where they reequipped with the new Armstrong Whitworth Whitley and in April 1938 returned to Yorkshire to be based at Linton-on-Ouse. A Whitley K8982 of No. 51 visiting Driffield on 22nd January 1939, skidded into a hedge on landing but was repaired on site. The No. 58 Squadron badge was awarded after it left Driffield.

By early 1937, most of the hangars and living accommodation at Driffield had been completed. The Sergeants Mess was designed on a basis that 50% of the SNCOs would be married and not use the mess. Creation of more Sergeant Pilots changed the situation and additional accommodation needed to be built. Some technical and domestic buildings were still hutted but permanent buildings in brick and concrete were built later to replace them as labour and materials permitted. About half of the initial cost budgeted of £515,000 had been spent by the end of March 1937- total cost had risen to £715,000 by end of March 1939. The 1937 Air Estimates for the first time exceeded those of the Army although Navy estimates were well ahead. At this time the Luftwaffe had at least 200 operational staffeln (squadrons).

The changes left No. 215 and 75 Sqns as the resident units through to July 1938. The squadrons could settle in to a routine but further massive changes were afoot in the Royal Air Force.

Driffield remained under the overall control of No. 3 (Bomber) Group H.Q. which had moved to Mildenhall aerodrome in Suffolk in January 1937, it was to take control of the aerodromes in the East of England. Then the 1st April 1937 saw the re-formation of No. 4 (Bomber) Group with its headquarters at Mildenhall but on the 29th June the Group Headquarters moved to the recently opened RAF station at Linton-on-Ouse. On the same day the Group took over Leconfield (Nos 97 & 166 with Heyfords), Finningley (Nos 7 & 76 Heyford and Wellesley), Dishforth (Nos 10 & 78 Whitley and Heyford), Driffield (Nos 75 & 215 Virginia and Anson). Linton's aircraft (Nos 51 & 58 Virginia and Anson) were based at Boscombe Down because of continuing construction at Linton-on-Ouse. No. 4 Group's headquarters moved to Heslington Hall, York on the 7th April 1940.

12th May 1937 saw the Coronation of King George VI. Empire Air Day was held on the following Saturday, 53 RAF stations with many civil aerodromes open to the public. These included Catfoss, Catterick and Thornaby plus the civil aerodromes at Brough and Hedon near Hull with Yeadon, the civil airport for Leeds and Bradford in Yorkshire. On 27th May Prime Minister Baldwin resigned in favour of Neville Chamberlain who had previously been the Chancellor of the Exchequer, he was to be Prime Minister of Britain until the early part of the war when Winston Churchill took over as Prime Minister of a coalition government.

The annual RAF Display at Hendon was held on 26th June with 260 RAF aircraft on show, this being followed by the Society of British Aircraft Constructors event at Hatfield on 27th and 28th. The public revelled in seeing the new types and large numbers of aircraft then coming into RAF service.

No. 215 was scheduled to re-equip with a mixture of Handley Page Harrow I and II which commenced 26th July 1937 with others arriving over subsequent months. Primarily they were the Mk II version with the more powerful Mk XX Pegasus engine whereas the Mk I had the Pegasus Mk X. Harrows had entered RAF service early in the year equipping No. 214 (B) Sqn at Scampton in Lincolnshire. Aircraft were painted in the dark green, dark earth and black undersides scheme with the squadron number on one side of the nationality roundel and an individual aircraft letter on the other side of the roundel. A few Harrow Is were received from Nos 214, 37 and 115 Sqns over the next year. No. 215 Squadron had its Badge awarded in November 1937 - *Surgite nox adest* - Arise, night is at hand, whilst at Driffield.

On 27th July 1937 the Operations Record Book discloses that two wooden huts which were part of the officers' quarters at Driffield, were burned out. The reason is not given. It is doubtful if actions taken by objectors to the growth in military forces or political reasons in other parts of the country could have affected Driffield but the cause could have been quite a simple one. The annual air defence exercises commenced on 9th August 1937 and a series of military interchanges between Britain and Germany continued to view each country's military manoeuvres.

Not all the aircraft to land at Driffield were bombers or even had the benefit of mechanical power! Phillip Wills with his glider *Hjordis* landed after a flight of 72 miles from Great Hucklow in Derbyshire on 3rd September 1937. The flight won him a prize from the British Gliding Association.

On the 13th September S/Ldr J.L. Kirby assumed command of No. 215, it had previously been commanded by Wg Cdr S.L. Quine MC (who had assumed command on 9th June) when he became Station Commander of Driffield. The squadron had completed its initial equipment of Harrow aircraft by 24th November. Wg Cdr Quine then resumed command of the squadron with S/Ldr Kirby taking over "B" Flight once again.

No. 75 Sqn was going to be re-equipped with the Harrow with the first delivered at the end of September, aircraft which had previously served with No. 214 (B) Sqn at Feltwell. Another batch arrived a month later from No. 37 (B) Sqn also at Feltwell. In later years, the squadron became known as the New Zealand Squadron within the RAF and the numberplate taken over by the Royal New Zealand Air Force. No. 75 Sqn lost an Anson on 28th October 1937, K6322 coded S. It had been delivered to No. 75 on 15th April 1937 and was piloted by P/O J.H. Pickering, the only occupant suffering injuries to his head and legs. During night-flying practice on approach to Driffield aerodrome, about a mile away he had to make a force landing at Elmswell, hitting trees. Another incident at about the same time involved an aircraftman who had been struck by a propeller receiving injuries to the shoulder and arm. He was taken to Catterick Military Hospital for treatment.

The building position in 1937 of RAF Driffield gauged from the 1938 site plan shows that all the Technical Site buildings were well underway to being completed although many of these were also mirrored by temporary hutted facilities, i.e.

A Driffield Heyford with a Whitley to the left.

(Yorkshire Air Museum)

During September 1938 all the RAF squadrons' aircraft were allocated "Munich" code letters to replace the squadron numbers. At Driffield No. 102(B) Sqn aircraft carried TQ as the Squadron code identification. The partially camouflaged Nos 4 and 5 'C' Type aeroplane sheds are in the background.

(Bill Jacobs)

Daladier of France. An agreement of consultation for peace was concluded and Chamberlain made the historic "Munich" declaration when arriving back at Heston on the 30th September giving Britain some breathing space.

The Armstrong Whitworth Whitley associated with Driffield by the early air raids on Germany and the eventful disastrous bombing of August 1940, had originated as a design in 1934 with the go-ahead for production in 1935. The first flight of the type took place at Baginton, Coventry on 7th March 1936 with the first production aircraft reaching No. 10 (B) Sqn at Dishforth near Boroughbridge on 9th March 1937. The Whitley was characerised during level flight by its nose-down attitude. The original marks of Whitley did not enter service with the Driffield squadrons as they received the Mark III which had an improved armament and Armstrong Siddeley Tiger engines. When the later Whitley Mk V version came along, these aircraft had the famous Rolls-Royce Merlin engines.

Whitley camouflage followed the new irregular pattern of matt dark green and dark earth to tone in with the landscape. Aircraft serials were in black against the camouflage with the unit number and individual letter usually in grey on either side of the roundel. The undersurfaces being black with large white individual aircraft serials below the wings.

The Munich crisis had caused the RAF emergency routine to be brought into force on 24th September and the formation of Mobilisation Pools ordered on 27th September 1938. A secret document SD109 gave details of mobilisation with the instruction that all operational aircraft were to be "toned down" and codes letters allocated to replace the squadron number. Various types of roundels succeeded the earlier type but it took time for the squadron numbers to be progressively removed. Each squadron was allocated a two letter code combination, all of these were changed upon outbreak of war in September 1939.

Aircraftman Bill Jacobs joined No. 102 Squadron at Driffield in November 1938 as a wireless operator with "B" Flight which was under the command of S/ Ldr Parker. He was later to attain the rank of Squadron Leader himself and has pointed out that the correct name of his initial rank was Aircraftman rather than the popular Aircraftsman! His operational exploits are related in a later chapter. At the time the squadron was converting from the Heyford to the Whitley and there was a shortage of flying personnel. His duties not only included flying but also the maintenance of the electrical and wireless installation on two Whitleys and also a Heyford.

A serious accident occurred to a No. 77 Sqn Whitley III K8963 which crashed at Dishforth on 24th November with one killed, P/O P. R. Wood, whilst the aircraft was destroyed by fire. Apparently the flaps had been raised too early. No. 102 also had its problems with the Whitley III all at Driffield, K8951 still coded 102.V had a landing accident on 17th November, K8946 hit an obstacle on landing (there were no runways then!) on the 22nd and K8949 belly landed on 28th following failure to lower the undercarriage, fortunately without any injury to the crew. The aircraft was repaired at Driffield and returned to service.

Bill Jacobs also had to perform station duties as Duty Signaller on a roster basis when night flying was being carried out. With the Duty Pilot (both would sit in the Watch Office) they were responsible for laying out the flarepath using gooseneck flares fed by paraffin. The gooseneck flare was originally used during the First World War and comprised of what appeared to be a small watering can containing paraffin with a wick of cotton waste in an elongated spout. The goosenecks were laid out to mark the limits of the grass runway in use and as dusk fell or the need arose had to be manually ignited. A Money flare (cotton waste soaked in paraffin in a stout wire basket) was placed at the approach end of the runway and ignited. Visual signals were given with an Aldis lamp fitted with red and green lenses. Aircraft had identification lights and reliance was placed on this visual communication between the pilot and the "flying control" organisation.

A 1938 plan was to extend the movement area at all bomber stations to provide a main strip of 1400 yards by 400 yards with subsidiary strips of 1100 yards by 300 yards. The heightening of tension during the year had also brought attention to the dispersal of aircraft. Whilst hangars were sited so that a direct hit on one should not affect another, aircraft were still kept in the hangars. Dispersal points were also to be provided with hard standings in fields adjacent to the aerodrome linked by a taxi track (some aerodromes had these camouflaged by grass!). The dispersals needed to be furnished with a shelter, in some instances a sunken Nissen hut earthed over and reached by a set of brick or concrete steps is known to have been installed at some bomber stations. The debate and progress with hard runways continued, Church Fenton the main fighter station for northern England was equipped with a main runway of 800 yards by 50 yards after it had opened (in 1937). Only Linton-on-Ouse was on the initial list of the Yorkshire bomber stations to have a hard runway.

Provision of ammunition storage had been foreseen under the Expansion programme Scheme F in 1936 which envisaged storage sites known as Air Ammunition Parks in the immediate vicinity of aerodromes to hold a week's war consumption of 750 to 1000 tons. The formation of Maintenance Command on 1st April 1938, brought four groups within the Command to control the supply of equipment, storage of aircraft, ammunition and fuel and finally the repair of equipment and aircraft. The first ammunition parks set up under Mobilisation Instructions September 1938 to service the Yorkshire bomber squadrons were No. 1 at Southburn (near Driffield) and No. 2 at Brafferton (near Ripon). Brafferton was an old First World War landing ground and located conveniently close to the A.1 trunk road. Southburn served Driffield and Leconfield with Brafferton serving Dishforth and Linton-on-Ouse. Finningley was served by No. 3 which was located in Lincolnshire at Swinderby (Norton Disney). Rail facilities were also essential and initially it appears that Lockington Station was projected for Southburn. The last lap of the journey to the operational bomber station would be by road transport.

RAF Southburn was sited about 1³/₄ miles to the South-East of the Driffield aerodrome Technical site. It had a branch track from the now disused LNER railway line from Driffield to Selby via Market Weighton. The camp buildings just to the south of Southburn Station and Wellsprings Drain comprised a guard room, station offices, barrack huts, ablutions, messes, air raid shelters and a decontamination centre. Two sites within the camp area accommodated armament storage with earth walls to deflect blast. It became No. 91 Maintenance Unit in October 1939 under the control of No. 42 Group, Maintenance Command. It acted as a holding area drawing supplies when needed from the main Ammunition Depot at Altrincham in Cheshire before being replaced by a new depot at Harpur Hill, near Buxton in Derbyshire. No. 91MU also had the responsibility of supplying oxygen as well as anti-aircraft shells to the Army units situated in the vicinity.

Southburn was camouflaged by using a plough land scheme. A number of satellites were opened, No. 1 was at Bainton Wood which by 28th August 1939 had three wooden barrack huts, messes, ablutions etc. in similar manner to the main headquarters site. Both High and Low Woods at Tibthorpe were used.

The disposition of No. 4 (Bomber) Group with its HQ at Linton-on-Ouse under the command of Air Commodore C.H.B. Blount on the 1st January 1939 included aerodromes with their squadrons at Dishforth, Finningley, Leconfield, Linton-on-Ouse and Driffield with the Station Commander Group Captain A. Lees, with No. 77 (B) Sqn Wg Cdr C.R. Strudwick and No.102 (B) Sqn Wg Cdr C.F. Toogood. Early in 1939 the two squadrons at Leconfield (Nos 97 and 166 still with the Heyford) became the No. 4 Group pool squadrons responsible for training crews - a task later organised into the Operational Training Units. Bill Jacobs spent a few weeks at Leconfield before going to No. 2 Air Observer School at Acklington for aerial gunnery training after which he received his gunner's identity badge of a winged bullet.

Early in 1939 Don Blew began training on the new Whitleys received by No. 77 (B) Sqn which also meant spending time with the School of Air Navigation at Manston for the Short Navigation Course. At the time all pilots were "dual purpose" there being no Navigator/Bomb Aimers. The nose turret on the Whitley was manned by an Observer/Bomb Aimer/Gunner which system continued until 1940. Don Blew was unfortunate in being shot down in May 1940 as related in Chapter 4.

Accidents continued to occur with a No. 77 Sqn Whitley III K8952 crashing about one mile north east of Driffield Aerodrome at Elmswell Wold on 20th February 1939 piloted by F/ O Caley who suffered slight burns. The rest of the crew were saved but the aircraft was destroyed by fire.

On 27th February after inspection by the No. 4 Group AOC, aircraft from Nos 77 and 102 flew to Northolt aerodrome near London to demonstrate the capabilities of the Whitley to an Arab delegation. Then a No. 102 Sqn Whitley III K8954 suffered an undercarriage collapse at Driffield on 22nd March but was repaired and returned to service. At the end of March various exercises were planned including black-out checks of the Firth of Forth area and with No. 12 (Fighter) Group, unfortunately bad weather caused the exercises to be cancelled,

Both Canada and Australia announced intentions to increase their own defensive forces. There had already been volunteers to serve in the Royal Air Force and during the war years many men along with a number of Dominion squadrons served at Driffield.

The 1st April 1939 saw the RAF celebrating its coming of age and the Air Ministry announced a scheme to improve the interest of the public in RAF squadrons. During the war this was used to coincide with the Wings for Victory Week and many towns "adopted" a squadron. Unofficially, No. 77 became "Lancaster's Own" and No. 102 "Morcambe's Own" and the adoption by these civic communities was for the purpose of raising war bonds.

regular basis to give the appearance of an active station, transport was provided some serviceable for the site crew to use and others were scrap vehicles and painted to look like the usual collection of MT on a normal RAF station.

To divert the enemy bombers at night "Q" sites were evolved using an elaborate system of lights to give the appearance of an active aerodrome. Runway and taxiway lights of the correct colours together with the approach funnel lights were turned on at the approach of hostile intruders and lights were used to mimic taxiing aircraft, some of the Night Decoy Sites utilised paraffin gooseneck flares to represent flarepath lights. The smaller number of staff required to operate a "Q" Site were housed in protected control bunkers. Driffield's "Q" sites were at Kilham, north of the Driffield to Bridlington road on the outskirts of Burton Agnes, and at Skerne immediately to the south-east of Great Driffield town. Throughout eastern and southern England there were about 200 decoy sites and those in No. 4 Group were headquartered at Linton-on Ouse at first and then at Heslington Hall, when the H.Q. of No. 4 Group moved.

The weather conditions in late 1939 were very bad with the aircraft flying into severe icing conditions that affected the Whitley's flying surfaces and propellers resulting in failure to maintain height and the control surfaces being jammed by ice. The cabin heating system was inefficient and the aircraft were extremely draughty and the crews wore a Sidcot Suit over a separate thick woolly "Teddy Bear" lining, under which would be their uniform tunic over a polo-neck sweater. Sheepskin flying boots and silk linings to their flying gauntlets with a leather flying helmet plus assorted leads completed the operational ensemble. Only the air gunners wore the electrically heated Irvine Suits and boots and they really needed them in their inhospitable environment. Many of the aircrew suffered frostbite on the long operational flights of that winter. In September No. 77 Squadron received ten of the new Whitley Mk.V from No. 78 Squadron at Dishforth and continued to be re-equipped through to October 1939. Don Blew's log shows that he flew Whitley V N1353, later KN.M, on the 16th. Six Whitley Vs were delivered on the 27th, 28th and 29th of the month and were allocated to "A" Flight, eight of their Whitley IIIs were then handed over to No. 102 Squadron. The Whitley Vs were initially issued to No. 78 Squadron where they were fitted out with operational equipment before handing them over to No. 77.

The latest version had liquid cooled in-line Merlin X engines and a Nash-Thompson power operated rear turret mounting four .303 machine guns, that had been given an increased field of fire by extending the rear fuselage by 15 inches. The new aircraft was an improvement on the previous Mk. III which was obsolescent on its introduction. Nos 77 and 78 Squadrons were the first of the No. 4 Group Whitley units to receive the new mark that had, in addition to the improved armament and engines, a ducted cabin heating system from the engines, an improvement in crew comfort, also wing leading edge de-icing rubber boots. The ventral turret was dispensed with from the Mk. IV. No. 102 Squadron re-equipped with the Mk. V from October 1939 and had a full complement by December.

December 1939 and a change in operational activity when three aircraft of No. 77 Sqn carried out the first daylight offensive sortie by Whitleys when they flew an anti-shipping sweep over the North Sea but no enemy shipping was seen. At this time a series of "Security Patrols" were started over the German seaplane bases on the islands of Sylt, Borkum, and Norderney. Minelaying seaplanes, Heinkel 115s, from these bases had been laying mines at night that were causing disruption to shipping in British coastal waters and the Admiralty requested the RAF to institute patrols to stop them operating. The bomber crews were under orders to bomb flarepaths on the water if lit and only to drop bombs in the water, they were still under the restriction not to bomb land targets. As a result the Whitleys were not allowed to bomb any of the islands that had a civilian population, the only island not in that category was Sylt. Don Blew in N1362 took part in one of these patrols over Sylt on the 12th/13th of December when nothing was seen and the sortie lasted six and a half hours.

A typical operation at this time was carried out by eight Whitleys from Driffield in the evening of the 19th of December with the objective of "destroying enemy mine laying aircraft taking-off or returning to Sylt and Borkum seaplane stations". The nature of these patrols is shown from the subsequent de-briefing. The patrol over Sylt and the seaplane base at Hornum was started at 1700hr on the 19th of December by N1375, DY.N from No. 102 Sqn which patrolled until 1840hr. A flarepath was seen to be lit on the water and six 250lb G.P. bombs were dropped on it. The next aircraft to patrol was N1382, DY.A, again from No. 102 arriving at 1930hr and staying in the area to 2115hr. The crew reported visibility of 30 miles but apart from two searchlights no activity. They were followed by N1373 from No. 77 Sqn which was on station from 2150hr to 2359hr and again although visibility was good nothing apart from some town lights were seen and no bombs were dropped.

The islands of Nordeney and Borkum are some 100 miles to the South-East of Sylt and the first Whitley in the area N1380, DY.R from No. 102 arrived at 1600hr and patrolled to 1805hr during which the crew reported anti-aircraft fire over Borkum and a flarepath alight on the water which was attacked with six 250lb G.P. bombs. Shipping including a destroyer was observed. The second patrolling aircraft N1415 from No. 77 Sqn arrived at 1950hr to stay until 2115hr again reporting ground anti-aircraft fire, one 250lb bomb was dropped on a ship. Next to patrol was N1357, KN.H also from No. 77 which patrolled from 2225hr to 0001hr and the crew saw nothing to report and no attacks were made. Another No. 77 Whitley N1367 followed from 0125hr to 0500hr, again apart from anti-aircraft fire and lights on the ground there was nothing to report and no attack was made.

The Driffield squadrons flew 34 sorties in the period 12th of December 1939 to the 25th February 1940.

John Grimstone was called up on the 29th of October 1939 and was accepted for training as a Wireless Operator/ Air Gunner and after basic training at Uxbridge and Finningley he was posted to Driffield on the 19th of January 1940 to join the Air Crew Pool. He recounts his arrival and early days there.

"That winter at Driffield was the bleakest I have ever experienced. We had snow drifts up to thirty feet along some of the hedge/ tree rows, and finally finished being completely cut off from the outside world. In fact we had to dig ourselves out along the road into the town , while a council team from Driffield dug toward us from their end, until they were able to supply us from their end with chocolate and other emergency "rations" by makeshift toboggans. We had survived on vegetables like swedes, dug from the surrounding fields.

We had also the job of clearing runways for the aircraft by shovel or just marching up and down. We cheered ourselves up with harmonica recitals in the billets. I had my *Larry Adler 64 Chromonica* with me and several other lads also played the harmonica. So much so that at one time we even formed a band with the backing of one piano-accordion. There were no ENSA shows in those days."

At the time it was essential that members of aircrew had an understanding of the morse code, and after it was found that John Grimstone had been a radio "ham" morse operator capable of 18 words of morse per minute he was "volunteered" to train the raw aircrew in morse up to the RAF standard of eight words per minute so they could signal by Aldis Lamp or with the aircraft's downward identification light in case of emergency.

In the same period Nos 77 and 102 Squadrons flew seven anti-shipping sweeps and also continued with *Nickelling* and by operating from an advanced base at Villeneuve they could now fly to Prague, Pilsen, Poznan, Warsaw and Vienna, as well as making the usual trips to the Rhur and other targets in Germany. On the 15th/16th of March two Whitleys of No. 77 released 6,000,000 leaflets around Warsaw.

The prototype Fairey Battle TT1, L5598, in 1940. The propeller drive to the target winch is on the port side of the rear cockpit and the stowage bin for the target drogues is located under the rear fuselage.

(Peter Green)

CONGRATULATIONS TO

CRACK 'EM&CO.

(THE HEROES, AND LEADERS, OF SYLT)

FROM AN ADMIRING DRIFFIELD

Driffield's visiting card distributed around Dishforth, the home of "Shiney 10" and No 51 Sqns after the raid on Sylt.

Fie Fie ! Oh Driffield,
You didn't have to tell us,
Honours lie easily on our heads,
You must be frightfully jealous.

But then you came in rather late,
Still—it must be galling,
To have your thunder stolen away,
We sympathise—It's appalling.

Rumours reach us of your navigation,
Spread by that lying jade ;
Of your "Drivers" hitting the wrong constellation,
Over Hunland—where a landing was made.

And there are tales of indiscriminate bombing,
On mackerel in the Great North Sea,
But we're nice and accept all these stories
With a large pinch of S.Y.L.T.

But we're BIG and we wish you the best of luck,
And when your next job is "on,"
Remember we'll always help you out.
Lots of love—10 and 51.

Dishforth's reply, printed on toilet paper, delivered by air to Driffeld.

(Colin Leadhill)

CHAPTER 5

THE BATTLE OF BRITAIN

After the fall of France Bomber Command continued the day offensive against aerodromes in France and Holland and night attacks against targets in Germany, although during the Battle of France the Command had lost 145 aircraft plus those that had crashed on return to home bases or had been damaged beyond repair, these losses represented half the front line force that had been available two months earlier at the start of the German Blitzkrieg.

Nos 77 and 102 Squadrons mounted 43 sorties over the last four nights of June 1940 against industrial targets in Germany for the loss of a Whitley P4948 from No. 77 shot down over the Ruhr on the night of the 29th/30th after attacking an alternative target at Essen.

After the evacuation of the Allied Expeditionary Force from the beaches and ports of northern France the German forces moved into the French aerodromes from where so recently the RAF had been operating. This proximity to the Channel permitted the Luftwaffe to make attacks against coastal convoys and heralded the start of the Battle of Britain as Fighter Command squadrons in the south of England were called upon to protect the convoys. In the north of England and in Scotland the squadrons recently returned from France had been distributed around many aerodromes to rest and re-equip. No. 88 Squadron arrived at Driffield with Fairey Battles direct from France (Moisy) on the 14th of June and stayed until the 23rd when it moved to Sydenham in Northern Ireland. During this period there is a reference to a Leading Aircraftman fitter "stealing" a Battle and flying it to Colerne in Wiltshire where he landed, was arrested and returned to Driffield to await disciplinary proceedings.

Driffield aircrews continued with night attacks against German industry and communication centres during the first week of July. The Germans were now beginning to assemble the barges for Unternehmung Seel we (Operation Sealion) by moving them through the canal system to the North Sea and thence to the captured Channel ports, at this stage attacking the barge movements was left to the day bombing force.

On the 4th of July a lone Junkers Ju 88 made an attack on RAF Driffield dropping five bombs that caused considerable damage to the wings of two airmen's barrack blocks and virtually destroying a block of Airmen's Married Quarters, water mains burst and electrical cables were also damaged. Fortunately only minor injuries were inflicted to 26 personnel, mainly by flying glass fragments, and only three were detained in hospital. No warning of any kind was received by the aerodrome before the attack.

The next day, one enemy aircraft bombed RAF Staxton Wold Chain Home (Radar) Station, on the northern edge of Yorkshire Wolds Escarpment to the south of Scarborough, at that time under the parentage of Driffield. RAF Staxton Wold was one of the first sixteen radar sites to be established in 1937 and became operational in 1939. It was still in use by the RAF in late nineties. The attack followed the pattern of the Luftwaffe attempts in the South of England to paralyse the RAF early warning reporting and control system. Four bombs were dropped and one airman was unfortunately killed but there was no material damage.

No. 102 Squadron joined in the anti-shipping strikes with participation by six aircraft in an attack against a battleship in port at Kiel on the night of 6th/7th of July. N1523, DY.B, failed to return from this mission, the five crew members being taken prisoner.

The "K" Decoy Site on the coast of Bridlington Bay at Skipsea was attacked by a single enemy aircraft on the 11th July. Five small bombs were dropped which fell about 50 yards from the nearest "K" aircraft (Whitleys) which were all undamaged. The craters were easily filled in by local RAF and Army personnel. No casualties were caused. Skipsea "K" site reverted to Catfoss control shortly after this raid.

Night bombing raids by the Whitleys of No. 4 Group continued on through July and into August with the Driffield aircrews involved on most of the raids. At the same time Blenheims were attacking aerodromes in France and Holland by day. One of the operations during August saw Flt Lt Learoyd earn the Victoria Cross during an attack on the Dortmund - Ems Canal by Hampdens of Nos 49 and 83 Squadrons, the first V.C. of the war awarded to Bomber Command.

Operations continued from Driffield when on the afternoon of the 14th nine aircraft from No. 102 flew to a forward base at Harwell, in Oxfordshire, from where overnight on the 14th/15th of August they bombed the Caproni Works at Milan and all returned safely. Twelve aircraft from No. 77 were despatched to attack an oil refinery at Bordeaux the same night and from this had their first loss in six weeks when a returning Whitley P5044 entered the Balloon Barrage defences around Southampton, hit a balloon cable at Eastleigh, and crashed with the loss of the crew. Another Whitley from No. 51 Squadron also fell victim to the Barrage Balloons this time at Slough.

Wg Cdr G.T. Jarmann took command of No. 77 Squadron and the next day Thursday the 15th of August 1940, the Luftwaffe mounted a major daylight attack against the North-East of England by Luftflotte 5 from bases in Scandinavia. At approximately 1000hr seventy Heinkel He 111s of KG 26 and twenty-one Messerschmitt Bf 110 took off from Stavanger in Norway en route for the Northumberland coast and various inland targets in the North-East including aerodromes. The twin engined Bf 110s were escort cover to the Heinkels and the range involved required the fighters to be equipped with under fuselage fuel tanks. About 0930hr a force of fifty Ju 88 from KG 30 took off from Aalborg in northern Denmark destined for the Yorkshire coast to attack RAF Driffield, a flight of some 500 miles. This latter raiding force had no fighter escort presumably expecting the defending fighters to be deflected from them by the northerly raiding force, and planned raids against the South of England. At about 1100hr the radar stations on the South Coast detected a large force of Junkers Ju 87 dive bombers and escorting Messerschmitt Bf 109 fighters forming up over the Pas-de-Calais that eventually attacked RAF Hawkinge, inland from Folkestone.

Anstruther radar station on the Scottish coast, to the south of St. Andrews, detected the northern incoming hostile raid and as a result of a navigational error the KG 26 aircraft were by now to the north of their intended track and it was assumed by No. 13 Group's fighter controller to be making for Edinburgh. The Heinkel crews realised their error and altered course to the south. At 1215hr Spitfires from No. 72 Squadron at Acklington were scrambled on a northerly vector, the Hurricanes of No. 605 at Drem took off at 1225hr to fly to the south-east, by 1235hr a further 25 fighters had been scrambled from Nos 41 and 79 Squadrons at Catterick and Acklington.

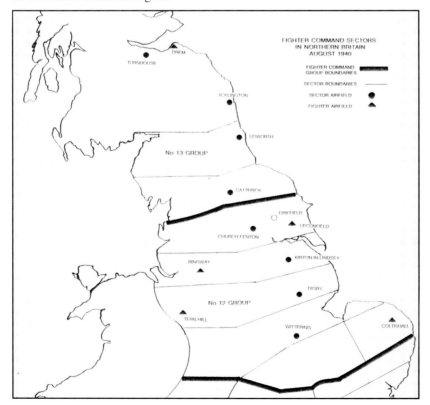

Fighter Command Sectors in Northern Britain. August 1940.

"Over at Eastburn Farm," *Tom Lawton* continues, " the dust had not yet settled before a truck with tin-hatted WAAFs arrived to assist. Good neighbours the RAF. They ran in a field telephone to talk to the aerodrome damage control, and calls for assistance - the post office lines were down - were sent through the RAF; for glaziers, tilers and the vet. We started to assess the damage. The Whitleys, at the corner, had been fully tanked and armed but were not bombed up or *I wouldn't be writing this*. They were burning and the ammunition was exploding. There were casualties amongst the ground crews, but the ambulances had already arrived. On the farm the house windows had been blown out and tiles shifted, one cow was dead, four injured, one horse had a badly damaged leg and another had shrapnel in it' hindquarters. One tractor driver had been hit by shrapnel."

An early arrival at the station after the raid was the Duke of Gloucester accompanied by General Ironside, they had watched the attack from a nearby Army H.Q. In his search for the Station Commander, in the ensuing chaos, the Duke was advised to move away from No. 2 Hangar as he was standing near an unexploded bomb that had penetrated the hangar door rails.

Two sources state that a No. 219 Squadron Blenheim Mk I, L8698, made a forced landing on Driffield after the pilot Sgt O.A. Dupee had been injured during an interception of a homeward bound Ju 88 over the sea. The Blenheim was flown to Driffield by the Air Gunner, Sgt Bannister, where he made a wheels up landing.

The RAF reported that Driffield after the raid was "damaged and disorganised" and assistance to the service personnel was despatched to the aerodrome by the local authorities in the form of two ambulances with first aid parties, a trailer fire pump and a motor fire engine. The number of bombs dropped during the raid vary, one source states 169.

On the "credit" side of the attack German sources give their losses as seven brought down over the land and into the sea plus three damaged aircraft that made it back to the Continent.

The actual track of the incoming raid, determined from people in the area who witnessed the raid, varies between passing to the north of and to the south of the town of Driffield and it may be that both are correct in that the Ju 88s would be have been spread out by the fighter attacks and in the distance flown from the coast would not have had the time or opportunity to regain a tight formation. Whilst the main track of the attack was to the north of the town, a two to three thousand yards spread, not unrealistic in the circumstances, would be sufficient to place aircraft on both sides of the town and create a difference in opinion of eye witnesses.

The final casualty toll amongst the station personnel was 13 killed, six RAF, one WAAF, six Army and one civilian. Three officers and eleven RAF other ranks and two civilians were detained in hospital with their injuries, five RAF personnel were slightly injured. The Military Plot in Driffield Cemetery has headstones for five of the raid's casualties.

In spite of the damage to its home base ten aircraft, five from each squadron were detailed to attack the Dornier factory in Augsburg the next night and one aircraft N1382 DY.A of 102 was shot down and crashed into the Walser Valley in Austria, with the loss of all five crew members. Four aircraft from No. 77 went to raid the Caproni works in Milan on the night of the 18th/19th and one of the Whitley crews claimed an enemy fighter shot down.

Following the August 15th raid a detachment of the RAF Regiment was moved in to augment the airfield defence force and were quartered in Eastburn Hall. Another raid by enemy aircraft on Driffield took place on the 19th of August, when one aircraft made a dive-bomb attack and No. 1 Hangar, which had so far remained undamaged, was hit. A direct hit through the roof removed the end doors and the ensuing fire caused considerable damage to the roof, the Driffield town fire brigade was summoned to help with the hangar roof fire and one civilian fireman was injured when he fell through the roof whilst firefighting. Jack Townend had been at Driffield from early in the month and his duties were in the main setting out the gooseneck flarepath at Cottam. He was at Cottam when the station was bombed on the 15th. He was back at Driffield on the 19th and recalls being in the shelter under one of the "H" barrack blocks. These barrack blocks had been built as protected units with basement refuges that were entered through a steel door and steps, under the barrack staircase, the refuge accommodated 40 airmen and a W.C. was provided. A 20ft long tunnel provided an escape exit.

The Driffield squadrons continued bombing missions despite the unwelcome attentions of the enemy air force to their home base and on the 24th/25th of August, 19 aircraft, ten from No. 77 and nine from No.

102 were required for operations. The No. 77 Sqn Whitleys went to attack the aircraft factory in Augsburg again and the No. 102 crews to bomb the Daimler-Benz works at Stuttgart. One aircraft N1473 from No. 77 crashed to the South-West of Haarlem in Holland with the loss of all five crew members. During that night whilst the Whitleys were over Germany the Luftwaffe carried out another attack on Driffield. This time by four bombers commencing at 0107hr, the raiders were heavily engaged by all the station defences, 12 bombs were dropped during three attacks at 0107, 0210 and 0238hr, a fourth attacker being driven off by A/A fire which damaged one of its engines. The Sergeants' Mess, already damaged, was reduced to ruins, David Waters was in the Mess that night and recalls walking through broken glass and also seeing people sheltering under the billiard table, one of whom was probably George Scott who admits to being in the Mess and taking shelter under the table. One Whitley received slight fabric damage, there were no listed injuries to personnel. The returning crews in the early hours of the 25th found the aerodrome cratered and damaged again.

On the 26th of August all the aircraft and personnel of No. 102 Squadron were moved to RAF Leeming and RAF Topcliffe was used for the dispersal of their aircraft. That night seven aircraft of No. 77 moved to the advanced base at Abingdon from where they attacked the Fiat works in Turin, all returned to Abingdon for debriefing and refuelling before returning to Yorkshire. Two days later, on the 28th, No.77 Squadron moved their Squadron Headquarters, flying crews and maintenance crews to Linton-on-Ouse, their aircraft to Tholthorpe and their Maintenance Flight to Topcliffe.

Following the August raids Driffield was closed for repairs for the rest of the year. No. 4 Group T.T. Flight was based at Cottam for about four weeks in September to October, (no reference is made to No. 5 Group T.T. Flight going with them, but it may be reasonable to assume that this was so).

Catfoss had reopened in August and the first unit to take up residence there was No. 2 (Coastal) Operational Training Unit, as a training unit for twin engined fighters and strike crews, with Ansons and one flight of Blenheim Mk.I. The OTU was a regular user of the aerodrome at Driffield from their arrival until some time in 1941, a report says that Driffield was used as it was kinder on undercarriages, but to which type was not reported.

A raid on Driffield by a formation of three enemy aircraft was made at 1800 hr on the 27th of October, practically no damage was done and no casualties resulted. A number of small calibre bombs were dropped and the station buildings were machine-gunned. One aircraft, a Ju 88A, was shot down by gunfire from the Station defence personnel. No warning was given and no defending fighters appeared.

formed at Linton-on-Ouse in February 1941, were flown in and the ground element followed by road. No. 5 Group T.T. Flight left Driffield for Coningsby in Lincolnshire at the beginning of April and its departure no doubt helped to ease the congestion around the camp.

Following the formation of No. 104 Sqn, No. 405 Squadron, the first Royal Canadian Air Force bomber squadron to form overseas, came into being at Driffield by the 23rd of April, and like No. 104 was equipped with the Wellington Mk. II. This squadron was a precursor of what was to become No. 6 (Canadian) Bomber Group whose squadrons were to be lodged on the airfields of North Yorkshire. With the formation of Nos 104 and 405 Sqns. Driffield was the only Wellington station in No. 4 Bomber Group until the formation of other RCAF squadrons during 1942/43.

No. 104 Squadron's operational debut took place on the night of the 8th/9th of May when six of its Wellingtons joined a major Bomber Command effort of 321 sorties against Hamburg and Bremen. The six Driffield crews attacked Bremen and Wilhelmshaven. This was followed the next night with six aircraft bombing Ludwigshaven, as part of a 146 bomber force attacking the neighbouring towns of Mannheim and Ludwigshaven. Wg Cdr W.S.P. Simonds assumed command of No. 104 with S/Ldr Beare in charge of "A" Flight and S/Ldr Cribb commanding "B" Flight. The latter was replaced almost immediately by S/Ldr Harry Budden.

F/Sgt Douglas Mourton, a WOP/AG, having completed his first tour with No. 102 at Topcliffe recounts having been posted to Driffield in May 1941. His duties at the new station were to instruct the No. 104 Sqn wireless operators who had just arrived and had no real knowledge of operational flying. Within two days of his arrival he was part of a Wellington crew, that was short of a WOP/AG, for a raid on Cologne!

This was the first time he had flown in a Wellington and he was deputed to be the front gunner. After climbing in to the front turret he realised that he was unable to get out, unless another crew member opened the door for him. He also left his parachute behind in the cabin. He admits it was a nerve-racking experience as he had already baled out once. On the previous occasion he was in the rear turret of Whitley N6236 DY.Q, on an op. to Turin on the night of the 23rd/24th of November 1940. After crossing the coast near Portsmouth the aircraft had been hit by friendly A/A fire. As a local airfield could not be seen the Whitley was abandoned at 0400hr to the north of Midhurst, Hampshire, and left to crash near Petersfield. Douglas now found being in the front turret of the Wellington an unpleasant feeling, and could imagine the crew baling out in a hurry and leaving him behind. He also felt utterly and completely unprotected and could not see what use he was in the front turret anyway.

He also recollects that he had moved his wife and future family to Driffield with him and had found lodgings in the town. He recalls a memory of rationing at the time whereby the whole household pooled their meat ration coupons occasionally so that a small joint of beef could be bought and a traditional Sunday roast with Yorkshire pudding could be enjoyed.

The Canadians lost one of their Wellingtons through enemy action on the night of the 4th of June when W5487 was destroyed by fire in an air raid on Driffield aerodrome. This was the first RCAF aircraft to be written off.

No. 104 Squadron took part in a bombing raid on the night of the 2nd/3rd of June when a force of 150 Wellingtons, Hampdens and Whitleys attacked Dussledorf. The No. 104 Squadron aircraft were led by S/Ldr Beare in W5438, EP.E, and carried loads of three 500lb, one 250lb HE plus 1440lb of 4lb incendiaries packed in six containers of 60. The target was obscured by some cloud at 500ft and ground haze. All the No. 104 Sqn Wellingtons returned safely.

No. 405 Squadron flew the first operational sortie by a RCAF unit on the night of June 12th/13th against the marshalling yards at Schwerte with four Wellington IIs each carrying a load of one 1,000lb, four 500lb and two 750lb canisters of incendiaries. All returned safely and claimed a successful mission but the crews had encountered ground haze at the target and later intelligence revealed they had not carried out a successful mission. The newcomers to ops were accompanied by No. 104 which had no more success.

On the night of the 16th/17th, No. 405 was again in action when Cologne was the target but in this case it operated from the newly completed aerodrome at Pocklington. From this raid No. 405, suffered its first loss on an operation when Wellington W5522, LQ.Q, failed to return and was presumed to have come down in the North Sea with the loss of the crew. This was the first bomber crew to be lost by the RCAF.

On the 20th of June the Canadian squadron moved into Pocklington and was the first unit to occupy this newly opened bomber station.

No. 4 Group T.T. Flt. was at Cottam again from May 1941, and in July carried out 16 air firing exercises, the flight left Cottam for the winter and returned to Driffield. On return it was re-designated No. 1484 Target Towing Flight, a change of title but the role for the newly titled flight was business as usual providing air gunner training for the squadrons in No. 4 Group using Fairey Battles to tow banner targets.

The Krupps Shipyard at Kiel was the target on the night of the 25th/26th of June and No. 104 was part of a force of 30 Hampdens and 17 Wellingtons to bomb Kiel. The same night an attack was made by 56 Wellingtons and 8 Whitleys on Bremen. On the Kiel bombing raid the No. 104 Squadron Wellington IIs were loaded with one 1000lb, four 500lb, two 250lb bombs and incendiaries. Haze once again affected bombing accuracy. Some of the Driffield aircraft suffered a variety of unserviceabilities, W5416 EP.A reported the front turret unseviceable on the way home and the rear turret would only move in jerks, the intercom in W5432 was u/s one hour after take off and W5485 EP.J, had one container of incendiaries hang up. All the No. 104 Sqn aircraft returned without loss.

Operations from Driffield continued with No. 104 Squadron taking part in the four months offensive against the U-boat manufacturing facilities in Germany and the two Battle Cruisers in harbour on the Bay of Biscay coast. No. 104 participated in the anti U-Boat offensive by attacking manufacturing targets in Germany losing its first aircraft W5513 EP.P, and crew during an attack by 85 aircraft on a rubber factory and the city centre at Hannover during the night of the 14th/15th of July.

On the 23rd of July reconnaissance revealed that the *Scharnhorst* had moved to new moorings at La Pallice some 200 miles to the south east of Brest. The squadron next participated in a daylight attack by 100 aircraft on the remaining battle cruiser, *Gneisenau*, in dock at Brest on the 24th of July. On this occasion the Wellington IIs carried eight 500lb SAP bombs, with S/Ldr Beare's aircraft loaded with one 2000lb and four 500lb bombs again all Semi-Armour Piercing. Wellington of No. 104, W5438 EP.E, was last seen being attacked by four enemy fighters and failed to return with loss of the crew. The crew of W5435 EP.F, flown by Sgt Huggins claimed a direct hit on the target. Another Wellington W5432, EP.H, flown by S/Ldr Budden was attacked by Bf 109s and with his navigator and rear gunner wounded, the elevators and rudder badly damaged and at one time on fire, he struggled back towards the English coast. On the way a lone Spitfire flew in formation with them. Out of ammunition, Harry and his crew were more than pleased to see their companion. What they did not know was that the Spitfire piloted by Ginger Lacey was as pleased to see them as he was also out of ammunition! Lacey recounts that the Wellington looked like a flying birdcage with its geodetic structure exposed. Harry Budden eventually succeeded in making an emergency landing at Exeter airport without flaps or wheels. The aircraft presented a dramatic appearance as all the fabric covering on the fuselage from the wings to the rear turret was missing. S/Ldr Budden received an immediate award of the DSO, his co-pilot P/O R.H. Sutton was awarded the DFC and his rear gunner Sgt J. Armstrong, who had stayed in his turret, whilst wounded,the DFM. Exeter Airport, close to the English Channel, was eventually opened as a diversion airfield by Bomber Command in 1942 so that injured crew members could be taken to hospital as soon as possible.

One of the characters around the camp at this time was Michael, a black and white spaniel belonging to Harry Budden. Michael had logged many flying hours including some over Germany. Sam Lawton (later Flt Lt DFC) remembers Michael sulking on the Crew Room table after being sent back from the aircraft by its owner and he also remembers the "pup" lying under the Wireless Op's table on a night trip to Brest. On the night of the 12th/13th of August, as the result of a last minute decision, Michael was left at Driffield whilst Harry went off to bomb Berlin. The Wellington W5461, EP.R, failed to return from this operation but the crew were safe, albeit prisoners of war.

An insight into the living conditions at Driffield is recalled by Sam Lawton who describes how aircrew were having to sleep on the floor of some of the empty Airmen's Married Quarters. Eventually, with his crew, he was billeted in the Rectory at Bainton, where the Rector and his wife had already provided a home to evacuee children. The crew's favourite drinking haunt was the Black Horse at the northern end of the town.

The Merlin X engines as fitted to the Mk II Wellington had the same short exhaust stubs as the Merlins installed in the fighters at this time and these glowed like beacons in the dark, not good when enemy night fighters are operating. Modified exhaust cowlings appeared and were hastily fitted. Although the modified cowlings shielded the glow from the exhausts the heat build up was intense so much so that the interior surfaces eroded and emitted a stream of sparks far astern for a considerable length of time much to the dismay of the crews.

and in the afternoon carried out organised games. No additional aircrew have reported to-day. P/O Eastwood proceeded to RAF Pocklington to take part in operational   sortie to Turin. Takeoff 1758hrs to 2135hrs. Landing back at RAF Abingdon.

19.11.42 Aircrew continued training in accordance with No. 4 Group Syllabus. 2 crews posted from 196 to 102 Sqdn. for flying duties.

20.11.42 Aircrew continued training in accordance with No. 4 Group Syllabus during the morning. In the afternoon all ground personnel and aircrew saw the film "Next of Kin" for security purposes. Total aircraft crews now on Sqdn. 17 + 2 on leave.

21.11.42 Aircrew continued training in accordance with the Syllabus issued by No. 4 Group. Aircraftman Standen wounded by a hand grenade during throwing practice and placed on the D.I. List, he was taken to Beverley Base Hospital.

23.11.42 Engineer Officer, P/O Griffith, reported for duty. Aircrew continued with training in accordance with Syllabus issued by No. 4 Group.

24.11.42 1015 P/O Montague E.H. Dawson, Navigation Officer, attended Buckingham Palace for a presentation of the DFM by H. M. the King. The DFM was awarded on 30th January 1942.
Aircrew continued training in accordance with the Syllabus issued by No. 4 Group in the morning and in the afternoon carried out organised games.

26.11.42 Aircrew continued with training in accordance with the Syllabus issued by No. 4 Group. 1415 A Gas Excercise was carried out by the Station, all personnel going to the shelters, with No 5 Anti-Gas Equipment, on receipt of the Gas Warning. Tear Gas and smoke bombs were dropped by aircraft on the Station.

27.11.42 1500 All ground crew attended a Lecture and Film by a Rotol expert in the NAAFI 1500 All aircrew attended a lecture by Wg Cdr Pleasance on enemy fighter tactics.

28.11.42 About 60% of the aircrew were sent on leave to-day, as no aircraft have been taken on charge, and this appears to be an ideal opportunity for leave to be taken. Remainder of crews on the training syllabus.

29.11.42 A request has been made by the Station Commander for aircrew to help local farmers to harvest root crops. This is being organised.

30.11.42 Aircraftman Standen removed from the D.I. List and placed on the S.I. List. Aircrew not on leave continued with training Syllabus. In the afternoon aircrew attended a film of " Air Fighting over Dieppe". No aircraft have arrived for the Squadron.

Not only the aircrew had to undertake training. During this setting-up period the ground crew members had also to be made familiar with their aircraft. To this end the whole of No. 466 Sqn "B" Flight ground crew was transferred to No. 196 Sqn where they were split into "A" and "B" Flights, at the same time the original "A'" Flight ground crew of No. 196 was transferred to No. 466 and split into two. Thus each squadron had two flights of ground crew where half of each had experience of the aircraft. When the squadrons had achieved operational readiness the ground crews reverted back to their original units.

1.12.42 Aircrew continued training as per Syllabus issued by 4 Group in the morning and in the afternoon took part in organised sport. Signals received today to the effect that 7 aircraft are to be delivered to this Squadron. 4 aircraft arrived p.m. to-day, 2 of these being Wellington IIIs and 2 Wellington Xs.

2.12.42 Aircrew attended a lecture given by Flt Lt Pipkin giving advice on actions to be taken in the case of a forced landing in enemy territory. Later a film on the Hercules 6 was shown. In the afternoon the ground training programme was followed.

3.12.42 2 Wellington IIIs delivered to this Squadron but were transferred to 429 Squadron at East Moor in exchange for 2 Wellington Xs . This was the first flying by this Squadron. Total aircraft on Squadron now 4 Wellington X's. 429 Squadron have 9 Wellington X's which are to be delivered to this Squadron at the earliest opportunity.

4.12.42 Weather unfit for flying, so the new aircraft could not be collected. In accordance with No. 4 Group instructions. 3 Pilots and Navigators went by train to Little Rissington and Ratcliffe to collect 3 Wellington IIIs for delivery to 429 Squadron at East Moor. Aircrew were engaged in organised sport during the afternoon.

5.12.42 4 new Wellington Xs delivered from East Moor and one Wellington III collected by East Moor. Crew training carried out in accordance with No. 4 Group instructions. Arrival of the new aircraft is causing severe congestion at Driffield, and the question of moving some aircraft to Leconfield is being investigated by the Wing Commander. Aircrew of "A" Flight returned from leave.

6.12.42 Arrangements were made for the movement of 1 W/O, 6 Sergeants and 97 other ranks to Leconfield. W/O Fairley was in charge of the party which left mid afternoon. P/O D. Wilson assumed the duties of Squadron Adjutant in the place of Flt Lt Sellers who had gone on leave.

7.12.42 4 Wellington Xs were flown to Leconfield in the morning, followed by 6 more Wellington Xs in the afternoon. Aircrew of "B" Flight due for leave proceeded on same. Ground training continued in accordance with 4 Group Training Syllabus.

8.12.42   2 further Wellington IIIs and 1 Wellington X arrived. Ground training was carried out by aircrew in the morning and organised games and P.T. in the afternoon. To date it has been impossible to carry out any air training because all the aircraft arriving at this Unit have had no valves in the intercom sets and it has not been possible to obtain a supply of valves.

9.12.42   The two Wellington IIIs which arrived on the 8th were flown to East Moor. Sufficient valves were obtained to equip the intercom of one Wellington X, and the intercomm was made serviceable in the afternoon. Aircrew continued with ground training. No flying apart from flying the 2 Wellingtons to East Moor was carried out.

10.12.42   In the morning a number of aircrew visited Pocklington to attend a lecture by a Naval Commander on " Mine Laying". No flying training was carried out due to unsuitable weather, aircrew continued with ground training.

11.12.42 Flying training still being held up due to lack of valves for intercom, but ground training carried out in accordance with 4 Group Orders.

12.12.42 Further aircrew, 3 only, arrived. This brings the total number of crews to 26 but 6 of these are without Bomb Aimers. The weather unsuitable for flying and ground training was carried out.

13.12.42 2 aircraft now have serviceable intercom sets, Circuits and landings were carried out by pilots. The shortage of valves is acute and is causing a hold up in flying training. Ground training carried out by other aircrew.

14.12.42 Further flying training carried out, mainly by pilots, but limited by the weather. 4 Group ground training carried out by non-flying personnel.

15.12.42 Weather unsuitable for flying, aircrew carried on with 4 Group Training Syllabus. In the afternoon the aircrew attended a lecture by the Station Signals Officer, this was followed by a talk on the work of the Pathfinder Force given by a Squadron Leader.

16.12.42 Flying personnel carried out flying training in the morning. In the afternoon aircrew attended a lecture by the Station Intelligence Officer and a second lecture by the Medical   Officer.   The Squadron Commander accompanied by the two Flight Commanders visited Leconfield preparatory to this Squadron moving to that Station on Sunday the 20th of December 1942.

17.12.42 Weather cancelled flying training. Ground Training Syllabus . W/O Mellor, who had attended an Engine Handling Course at Bristol gave a lecture to the aircrew.

18.12.42 No 4 Group Training Syllabus carried out by aircrew during the morning. In the afternoon 196 Squadron played 466 Squadron at football the final result being 196 Sqn - 6 goals and 466 Sqn - 3.

19.12.42 No flying due to weather, 4 Group training Syllabus carried out. The Squadron move to Leconfield planned for 20th December has been postponed to Tuesday the 22nd of December.

20.12.42 Movement Order for Squadron distributed to all concerned. Flying training carried out but cancelled after 1´ hours due to the weather. Ground training continued for the rest of the day.

Note. The Station ORB for Driffield states that Leconfield was taken over as a satellite for Driffield on the 20th of December 1942.

21.12.42 Aircrew carried out ground training and also completed 9 hours flying training.

22.12.42 The Squadron moved to Leconfield by air and road transport to-day. The road party moved off at 11.40hrs. The air party took off at 1500hrs.

It was planned to close Driffield at the end of 1942 for reconstruction and No. 466 left in appalling weather conditions to join No. 196 at Leconfield. No. 466 were to return to Driffield eighteen months later with the Halifax B.III.

Driffield was then closed down as an operational bomber aerodrome, but remained active with the Air Fighting Development Unit, Nos 1484 and 1502 Flights.

During the time that Driffield had been out of the front line of Bomber Command operations there had been major changes in aircraft with the introduction of the latest four engined bombers. Crew comfort was much enhanced with the issue of combination underwear for flying. Made of fine wool the long-johns were both warm and comfortable so that aircrew no longer required the bulky Sidcot Suits with wooly linings although the gunners still wore electrically heated suits, flying boots and gloves. The aircraft now had better heating systems giving increased crew comfort. Creature comforts were also improved with better flying rations and if the individual was unfortunate enough to find himself on the ground in enemy territory escape kits were now issued. In the early days of the war the only escape assistance provided were silk maps sewn into the shoulder pads of the tunic, but with the issue of battle dress shoulder pads disappeared. A magnetised fly button was also sewn onto the trousers which was marked with a white spot and when suspended by a thread indicated north. The escape kits were now packed in flat clear boxes, 6 inches by 4 inches and $3/4$ of an inch thick, containing the silk maps, money, concentrated malted milk tablets, water purifying tablets , a small water bottle and Benzedrine tablets. The kits were issued pre-operation and returned at debriefing. One other escape aid was the latest flying boot in which a sheepskin lined shoe was stitched to calf length zipped upper, again sheep skin, a knife was concealed in the upper to allow the evader to remove the leg part and convert the flying boots into a close approximation to civilian shoes.

There had been changes in command of No. 43 Base at Driffield following the replacement of Air Commodore Walker by Air Commodore Whitley who had been promoted from Station Commander at Lissett. The Station Commander at Driffield, Gp Capt Tom Sawyer DFC, was posted to Lissett to command. Wing Commander D.T. Forsyth DFC, an Australian who had been the No. 466 Squadron Commanding Officer since September 1943, was promoted to Group Captain and Station Commander at RAF Driffield. The command of the squadron passed to another Australian, Wing Commander H.W. Connolly DFC.

The Australian squadron was soon into action from Driffield attacking the gun battery at Maisy which overlooked the beaches code named Utah and Omaha, soon to be the scene of the American landings on the Normandy coast, as part of Operation Overlord. The bomber crews had not been briefed about the impending invasion but as they made their return trip in the early hours of the 6th of June the crews witnessed the huge invasion armada crossing the Channel beneath them.

Bomber Command's effort following the invasion was to support the Allied armies in France with attacks against military targets, communication centres and airfields. During this phase No. 466 lost their first Driffield based Halifax MZ283 HD.F, in an attack by a mixed bomber force of 337 aircraft against rail targets at Juvisy, just to the south of Versailles on the night of the 7th/8th of June. As the targets were further from the battlefront German night fighters were active and the loss rate for the night was 8.3% of the bomber force. Apart from the losses due to enemy action accidents during training flights were still showing that flying is a dangerous occupation and a No. 466 Halifax MZ305, delivered to the squadron a month earlier, and operating from Leconfield, took off on the 14th of June for a cross-country training flight and an hour and a half later crashed at Meopham Green near Gravesend with the loss of all on board.

A typical day at Driffield, and probably most other bomber squadrons, is recalled by Alby Silverstone (RAAF) a F/Sgt Bomb Aimer with No. 466 Sqn.

"Life on the squadron was quite different to anything we had experienced elsewhere in the Air Force although the routines were fairly simple. Each flying category had their own sectional office. If you had flown the previous night you were required to report to your section by 1400hr having spent the earlier hours sleeping and eating. If you had not flown you were required in the appropriate section by 0900 hr.

The Pilot group had a Flight Commander with a Squadron Leader in charge of each Flight, usually two to a squadron. The other sections had a different ranking but appropriately named officer in charge of their respective groups such as Navigation Officer, Bombing Leader, Signals Officer, Engineering Officer and Gunnery Leader. He was often a Flight Lieutenant, a member of a senior crew and at that point often an officer engaged on his second tour of operations.

Upon reporting to Section the airmen concerned filled in the time in many and varied ways. Firstly, it was time to meet other similarly graded men and learn each other's experience first hand. Secondly, it was time to seek advice on any flying problem that may present. Thirdly, you could read any official literature that was available. Sometimes this was technical, sometimes theory and at other times simply stories of events such as raids.

All signals concerning operations and crews involved were promulgated in the Flight Office. The pilot was therefore the first to know if he was listed; this was usually a sign for him to contact his crew with the time of briefing. The signal from Group Headquarters came through daily and advised if "ops" were on or if the squadron had been stood down. Amongst other things, the signals would indicate the size of effort required, i.e. the number of crews and bomb loads. These and other details such as target and bombing times were passed to each squadron in great secrecy over scrambled teleprinter lines and once a raid was known to be scheduled all aspects of station life went under a security wrap, a complete communications blackout. No persons were allowed on or off the station and all private telephones went off the air.

When the station was not required for flying all aircrew would be stood down and from then until normal reporting time of the next cycle, were free to pursue their own interests. Each airman was deemed to have a permanent leave pass for all periods of stand down, provided that they were back at the station fit and well when required. It was expected that all personnel be contactable if required urgently. Usually crews stood down merely went to the nearest town, in our case Beverley whilst at Leconfield, and later, after we moved stations, Driffield. Crews seldom went further afield unless there was a general close-down because of fog, snow etc.

Once an operation was signalled the whole might of the station started to roll particularly Armaments, Intelligence and Catering. Briefing always started punctually and crews were always early because, once all was ready to commence the doors were locked and latecomers were placed on "open arrest" for subsequent charges. All crews reported en masse and took up seats in a large briefing room which was capable of seating 250 persons. The seated crews faced a raised dias which featured a giant backdrop on which was a large map of Europe always covered by a curtain at briefing time. All the section leaders would be seated on the dias.

Exactly on time, usually about $2^1/_2$ hours before take-off time, the Station Commander and Squadron Commander would enter and mount the dias, while at the same time the Service Police would shut and guard the doors. The Squadron Commander would invariably start the same way: "The target for tonight is .... "and the Intelligence Officer would pull back the curtain and reveal the target and proposed route. The C.O. would generally merely point out the target with some simple comments and then pass on to the various specialist officers.

The Navigation Officer would detail the route to be followed, the heights to be used and the latitude and longitude of the various turning points. The Intelligence Officer would give a fairly lengthy talk on the target to be attacked, alternative targets and the defences that might be expected en route and on return. The Bombing Leader would then speak on the bomb load, its size and placement on the aircraft, the order of release to be set, the armouring details such as size, weight, detonation delays and purpose of the bomb load. He would finish with the Pathfinder Force, details of visual signals to be used, the type of target markings to be expected and the PFF code words to be used.

The Signals Officer would then give details of the wireless and R/T channels to be used, the IFF (Identification Fried or Foe) channels and the ground channels of the day. Where necessary, he also gave details of any special signals that might be expected, such as wind or weather changes, and Window foils to be expelled by the wireless operator.

The Gunnery Leader usually spoke on the armament carried on board and the briefing would finish with time of take-off, the wave formation, the set course time, the bombing time, the time of the flying meal and a general time check.

Immediately after briefing the navigators went off to their Section Office for detailed discussion of the route and to collect various maps, charts and flying aids they would need such as sextants, hand computers, astro conversion tables, protractors, log sheets etc.

All crews then went to "flying breakfast" usually a hearty meal consisting of steak and eggs. After breakfast they went back to their quarters and looked after any personal matters, locked away all personal effects from their pockets and selected their flying equipment with care. The rear gunner usually wore a full flying suit but the rest of the crew only added heavy flying jumpers, heavy socks, flying boots, gloves and helmets.

The final action before boarding the crew buses was a visit to the parachute store for parachutes, emergency rations and escape kits. The buses usually left about thirty minutes before take-time and this gave the crews time to talk to the ground staff, have a last cigarette and go through their warm up drill".

Halifax force. The attack cost the Halifax squadrons 17 aircraft including NP969 HD.Q. Following the Magdeburg raid the weather inhibited offensive activity and No. 466 were not operational until the 22nd/23rd of January when fourteen Driffield crews went, without loss, as part of a small area attack on Gelsenkirchen by 152 aircraft. The next trip was as part of the two pronged attack on the Stuttgart area when No. 466 attacked the marshalling yards at Kornwestheim, a town to the north west of Stuttgart. The first three operations in February were against Mainz, Wanne-Eickel and Gelsenkirchen and in all three attacks the targets were obscured by cloud and bombing was on sky-markers and on the latter two by Gee fixes.

On the night of the 7th/8th of February Bomber Command was again involved in a tactical operation when it was to pave the way for the British XXX Corps advance across the German frontier. The towns of Goch and Kleve had been fortified by the Germans and were on the advance front to the Rhine and the northern Rhur. No. 466 sent eighteen crews as part a force of 292 Halifaxes, 156 Lancasters and 16 Mosquitoes. The cloud base was low, about 5,000ft, and the Master Bomber ordered the crews to attack from below the cloud base. After about 150 bombers had attacked the bombing was stopped as smoke was making accurate control of the raid impossible. During the raid one crew from No. 466 claimed a Messerschmitt Me 410 destroyed. The next night a return raid was made on Wanne-Eickel.

A notable feature of the operations now being mounted by Driffield was the number of aircraft involved on each raid, in general these were now about fifteen and had been since the Halifax arrived. A huge increase since the Whitley days when the commitment rarely reached double figures. Apart from the number of aircraft involved the quantity of aircrew was vastly different, whereas the Whitley had on average five in a crew and the Wellington six now the Halifax had normally seven, and, eight if a co-pilot was on board. The aircrew commitment from No. 466 in the Goch raid was 126 individuals.

For some time the Air Ministry had been considering carrying out heavy area raids on German cities in an attempt to break down the German war machine and civil administration, these raids were part of the plan known as Operation Thunderclap. The implementation of the plan had been delayed until the military situation was considered to be right. Targets selected behind the German lines on the Eastern Front were Berlin, Dresden, Leipzig and Chemnitz and were all vital communication and supply centres. The Russians had asked at the Yalta Conference for such air attacks to be made. The first raid under Operation Thunderclap was against Dresden on the 13th/14th of February by a Lancaster force plus nine Mosquitoes followed by another Lancaster attack three hours later. The same night No. 466 sent thirteen aircraft as part of a Halifax raid on the synthetic-oil plant at Bohlen, near Leipzig, a long sortie of nearly 9 hours, one No. 466 Halifax had trouble with icing and short of fuel landed in France at Juvincourt. Chemnitz, now Karl-Marx-Stadt, was the next Operation Thunderclap target for nearly 500 Lancasters and 218 Halifaxes which included fifteen from Driffield on the 14th/15th, fuel shortage resulted in some aircraft landing away from base. The synthetic-oil plants were again the targets for No. 466 on the 20th/21st and the 21st/22nd.

February closed with attacks on Essen, Kamen and a daylight raid on Mainz on the 27th. No. 466 Squadron lost no aircraft during the month.

Cologne was attacked in daylight on the 2nd of March by 531 Lancasters, 24 Mosquitoes and 303 Halifaxes which included fifteen Driffield aircraft. This was probably the most destructive raid on this target where specific targets were the Rhine bridges and ferries. Cologne was taken by the American troops four days later.

The Luftwaffe had long planned a major intruder mission under the code name Operation Gisela against the bomber bases in Yorkshire, Lincolnshire, Norfolk and Suffolk. The German night fighters struck back at the RAF bombers in the early hours of the 4th of March as they returned to their bases. The Lancasters had raided Ladbergen and the No. 4 Group Halifaxes had made a successful attack on the Fischer-Tropsch synthetic-oil plant at Kamen. Ju 88s took off from bases in Holland and Germany to follow the bomber stream by flying beneath the returning bombers. The German night fighters were under orders not to attack over the North Sea. At Driffield eleven aircraft had landed safely and the other six were still airborne. NR250 HD.N fell to an intruder at about 0040hr, the crew baled-out but there seems to be doubt as to precisely where the Halifax crashed. NR179 HD.C, arrived at Driffield and the crew were told to circle at 1,700ft with the navigation lights on dim. Later the aircraft was called down to 1,400ft and finally told to prepare to land, however on making the approach the pilot was denied permission to land and an overshoot was carried out. Another circuit was performed and landing permission was given. When the Halifax was at about 150ft altitude all the airfield lights were extinguished and the pilot was instructed to fly a "dog leg". The aircraft then set off on a course for Pocklington. Advised that only 15 minutes of fuel were remaining the pilot climbed to 4,000ft so that the crew could bale-out if necessary. A Ju 88 was seen to be approaching from below to the left, the Halifax was attacked and set on fire at about 0110hr. The navigator, mid-upper gunner and rear gunner escaped by parachute, although at low altitude, but the flight engineer who left last was too low for his 'chute to deploy properly and he and the remainder of the crew were killed. The Halifax crashed at Fridaythorpe to the north west of Driffield. In addition to the two No. 466 aircraft shot down by the intruders, twenty three Halifaxes and Lancasters and one RAF Fortress were lost to the intruders that night including some from HCUs. The records show that twenty five Ju 88s were lost during Operation Gisela.

Driffield crews were again on ops on the night of the 5th/6th against Chemnitz, one of the Operation Thunderclap objectives. The bomber force comprised 1100 aircraft of which fifteen were from No. 466. Severe fire damage was caused and a tank factory was destroyed. Icing conditions over Driffield were bad and as a result one No. 466 pilot lost control of his aircraft, baled his crew out, and eventually regained control at 2,000ft, and then made a safe emergency landing at Carnaby. Another No. 466 Halifax suffered severe control problems and returned to base after about three hours. This aircraft, MZ914, made a safe landing but was declared beyond the local repair capability, the Halifax remained at Driffield until the 12th of April 1945 when it was struck off charge. Bomber Command lost a total of 41 aircraft in operations during the night of the 5th/6th of March, nine were lost by No. 6 Group shortly after take off due to icing conditions over North Yorkshire, one of which crashed on York killing some civilians.

On the nights of the 7th/8th and 8th/9th of March the oil refinery in Hemmingstedt and the Blohm und Voss shipyards at Hamburg were attacked. In each raid No. 466 participated and on the latter eleven crews were despatched against the U-boat assembly yards where the latest models were being built.

At this stage of the war the Rhur was being threatened by the advancing armies on two fronts and an attack by 1,079 aircraft was made on Essen in daylight on the 11th with similar sized raids by the USAAF on Hamburg, Bremen and Kiel at the same time. No. 466 sent fourteen aircraft to Essen without loss. The next day saw a similar raid on Dortmund. After the daylight operations it was back to night bombing for the Driffield airmen on the 14th/15th, 15th/16th and 18th/19th. These were followed by a daylight attack on the railway yards at Recklinghausen on the 20th and again the next day to a similar target at Rheime when twelve Driffield crews took part. From these operations all No. 466 aircraft returned, but on the Rheime attack nine of its aircraft were damaged by the accurate flak. The month of March closed for No. 466 with daylight attacks on Gladbeck on the 24th and Munster on the 25th.

By the beginning of April 1945 the war in Europe was drawing to a close and No. 466 were only to participate in five more missions. The first of which was to the oil refineries at Harburg on the night of the 4th/5th followed the next night with an attack on the U-boat yards at Hamburg. For this operation the crews were briefed to fly east across the North Sea to make a landfall on the German/Danish coast near Sylt and then to head South-East and due south to Hamburg to attack from the north. The return route briefed was south to Hanover, then South-West to Munster and on to the Ruhr, now in Allied hands. The route was then on to the Scheldt estuary and north-west to cross the Yorkshire coast near Whitby and then home to Driffield. NP968 HD.B, from No. 466 was over the target between 2230 and 2240hr dropping ten 500lb ANM64 and four 500lb HC bombs and two packets of leaflets. At approximately 2300hr HD.B was shot down by a night fighter. Six of the crew exited the aircraft by parachute but one, the navigator, was never heard of again and the pilot never left the aircraft. The WOP/AG landed safely and was on the run for 13 days before being captured to be released a few days later by a patrol of the Scots Guards. On the same raid LW172 HD.F (formerly coded J), on its 97th operation was severely damaged and on return to Driffield the airfield was fogbound. Most of the other Squadron aircraft had been diverted but the pilot of LW172 said he could make it but unfortunately the aircraft crashed in trees on Kirkburn Grange Farm some two miles to the west of the aerodrome. Conditions were so bad on the ground that the crash crew were led to the scene by a Driffield airman, with local connections, on a bicycle riding in front of the fire engine. The Halifax had disintegrated and there were no survivors. The previous night this crew had fought off an attack by a Me 410 whilst crossing the Dutch coast.

These were the last aircraft to be lost from Driffield on wartime operations.

The final three raids to be flown by No. 466 were to Nuremburg on the 11th of April to attack the railway yards when all the Halifaxes on the raid were led by No. 466. Again, on the 18th when nearly 1,000 bombers attacked the airfield and naval base on the island of Heligoland. Following the Heligoland raid Driffield had not operated for a week and being convinced that the war was as good as over, a mess party was organised on the evening of the 24th and F/O Don Otten recalls getting to bed at around 0430hr on the 25th, much the worse for wear. He was roused at 0930hr by the WAAF bat-women and advised he was required

PG238 of No. 228 OCU at Leeming overshot during a single engine landing at Driffield.

Greville Jacques like many other pilots did his training overseas and completed his first operational tour in Italy during the Second World War coming back to the UK for refresher flying at Coleby Grange in Lincolnshire and Beam Approach training at Wheaton Aston in Shropshire. He was then as a Flying Officer posted to No. 10 ANS Driffield in April 1947 joining Staff Pilot Training Course No. 6. After an introductory flight as second pilot in Wellington T.10 NA968 with Flt Lt Hoad he did a dual conversion flight with Flt Lt Don Thieme in Anson T.1 MG859 as part of the course work. Flying a number of solo flights in MG859 and NK948 he did circuits and landings and then as pilot took over Anson MG830 carrying out navigation details for two pupils during the last few weeks of April.

Similar flying was done throughout May and June with various Ansons, some flights over three hours (day) along with some dual instruction given to him at night by F/O Jackson on LV280 and MG629. This qualified Greville Jacques to fly at night providing navigation instruction for pupils. Some weekends he was able to cut from the Officers' Mess and walk into Driffield, board a train for Hull en route for York and London to meet the future Mrs Jacques and dash back for flying early Monday morning.

In July he received conversion training on Wellington T.10s NC858 and RP545 followed by a similar schedule to that on the Anson before qualifying as a Staff Pilot at the end of July and moving on to No. 1 ANS at Topcliffe. His service life eventually lead to helicopter training where a tour in the Far East was done flying Dragonfly helicopters in the Casualty Evacuation Flight as well as Auster aircraft of No. 656 Squadron. After leaving the RAF as a Flight Lieutenant, Greville Jacques began civil flying with Silver City Airways and Autair and taking up helicopter flying in the mid 1950s both in the UK, Greenland, Antarctica and India before retiring from flying.

A Battle of Britain day was held on 20th September 1947 which had formation flying by Wellingtons and Ansons of the school. The fly past included Lancasters, Spitfires, Mosquitoes and Miles Masters. About 2000 people attended.

Derrick Milner who was previously a WOP/AG came to Driffield as a Staff Wireless Operator (later known as Signaller) with No. 10 ANS in October 1947. Exercises were carried out often of a three hour duration in Ansons LT122 coded FFT-O, MG616 coded FFT-F and "298" (likely MG289) coded FFT-A. These were to give instruction in navigation, radio procedures, using radio bearings for homing back to base and even bombing detail! Several pilots conducted Derrick around the country on these flights including, Flt Lt Budd, F/O Mersh, F/O Palmer, W/O Adamek, F/O Yarrington, Flt Lt Griffiths, W/O Pietrzyk, F/O McPherson, P II Mann and P II Davies with different pilots later on indicating the pool of pilots which was available for duty. Over the next few months exercises were carried out in other Ansons and also in the Wellington T.10 RP545 coded FFS-K featuring on a number of occasions. The Wellington cross country flights were of a much longer duration being up to six hours (day) and 3 ´ hours (night).

On the 19th January 1948 during a flight in Anson LT978 coded FFT-D, piloted by Flt Lt Budd on a night detail cross country having completed three and a half hours flying they got diverted to nearby Leconfield as an Anson had "pranged" whilst landing at Driffield.

Training was completed by the end of February 1948 and concluded with Derrick as Staff Wireless Operator on a passenger flight with P II Davies to Spitalgate in Anson LT978. By this time No. 10 ANS was just about ceasing to exist, its role being transferred to No. 1 ANS at Topcliffe where Derrick was posted, he later moved on to fly as a Signaller in Lincolns.

On 12th December 1947, a formation of ten Blackburn Firebrands landed at Driffield. They had been on a flight routing from the aerodromes at Acklington in Northumberland to Culdrose in Cornwall via Lakenheath in Suffolk. Poor weather caused a diversion to Driffield and the following day the squadron left for Lee-on-Solent in Hampshire. The squadron is highly likely to have been No. 813 Sqn serving with Naval Aviation of the Admiralty (it was not until May 1953 was it renamed to the earlier title of the Fleet Air Arm). About this time the squadron was in transit from Lossiemouth to its new home at Culdrose after being afloat on HMS Implacable. The Firebrands had been built at the nearby Blackburn aerodrome of Brough and as the Torpedo Fighter Mk V equipped No. 813 Squadron between April 1947 and August 1953.

The New Year opened with the loss of Anson T.1 MG672 on 19th January. It crashed hitting the railway embankment on a night approach to Driffield resulting in the aircraft being struck off charge, the extent of damage not being recorded but it is known that consideration to the cost of repair would be taken into

The signallers "office" in the Anson I.

(Derrick Milner)

The Watch Office and Control Tower at Driffield in post war paint finish. No. 3 hangar in the background.
(Hull Daily Mail)

Possibly the first fatal accident involving a No. 203 AFS Meteor occurred on 15th November when VW448 crashed at Kirkburn having flown into fog after take-off and hit an obstruction. Unfortunately, over the next four and a half years quite a number of accidents occurred with the loss of several lives, many during single-engine approaches which were practised as part of the flying training syllabus.

A ground based unit at Driffield was the Air Crew Transit Unit which moved from Digby in December 1949. Pupil pilots were posted to the unit when they had completed their initial ground studies. In January 1950 some 112 cadets, 11 officers and 31 trained aircrew personnel passed through en route to Initial Training School at Wittering or Digby. The unit remained at Driffield until the end of 1951 when it moved to Cranwell. Terry Holden came to Driffield as a National Serviceman who had volunteered for flying. He recalls being posted to Driffield for "holding" in November 1950 prior to basic flying training at Ansty near Coventry. Most of the time was spent on barrack cleaning, cross country running and general keep fit courses but they did receive instruction on service discipline. The pay was £1 per week and during his time remembers seeing crashed Meteors on the airfield. They lived in a Nissen hut but he was at Driffield for only a few weeks before moving to start his basic flying training. Instead of coming back to Driffield after achieving his "wings" he went to No. 205 AFS at Thornaby-on-Tees near Middlesbrough for his jet training. Then he went to No. 226 OCU at Stradishall before joining No. 64 Sqn on Meteors at Duxford in Cambridgeshire. He was later to fly with No. 613 (City of Manchester) Squadron Royal Auxiliary Air Force and continued his flying after its disbandment in 1957 with various cadet Air Experience Flights.

Driffield was short of aircraft parking space by the hangars - the wartime dispersals now out of use being too far from the operating area. A large concrete apron was proposed and included in the 1950 Air Estimates, between Hangars No. 3 and No. 4 and a smaller one north of Hangar No. 4 for starting up and parking . It was built between July and September 1950 facing the hangar line along with an Operational Readiness Platform at each end of the main runway which remained at 6000 ft long and 150ft wide. To enable this work to be carried out the flying activities of No. 203 AFS were transferred to Carnaby.

On 2nd August 1950 H.Q. Flying Training Command notified Driffield that it was earmarked as a Fighter Command deployment station and steps may be taken to provide a parallel runway. Possibly this had something to do with Plan Galloper which involved the United States bringing over extra aircraft to the UK in the event of a serious emergency. This had been devised in July 1950 and several UK airfields were inspected including a number of those which were disused for flying but kept in readiness. A sighting study was carried out and a site chosen to the north of the existing 06/24 runway with details submitted to Fighter Command on 12th August. The choice was narrowed and Driffield was not selected and even the idea of a parallel runway at the other bases was not developed.

On 16th September, Driffield participated as a Battle of Britain "At Home" station receiving 7000 visitors to view the display given by No. 203 AFS, a static park, formation flying and also a demonstration of the Martin-Baker ejection seat ground trainer, one of the first in the hands of the RAF at the time. A service of remembrance was held in Driffield parish church the next day and the local branch of the Royal Air Forces Association laid a wreath.

Accommodated for a short time at Driffield was No. 264 Squadron equipped with Mosquito NF.36. Based at Coltishall in Norfolk, they had been detached to Church Fenton whilst repairs and improvements were carried out at Coltishall. They moved from Church Fenton on 2nd October for Driffield to participate in Exercise Emperor. At this time the squadron used a "shadow" squadron numberplate as No. 264/79 Squadron. Exercise Emperor was held between the 7th and 15th October and was the UK annual air defence test. It also enabled the B-50 Superfortresses of the United States Air Force Third Air Division to carry out simulated bombing runs over Britain from the Continent. These were carried out as both day and night "raids" on several occasions against docks and industrial targets. The aircraft operating out of Driffield completed 48 sorties claiming 54 night kills and received the congratulations of Yorkshire/North Eastern Sector of Fighter Command. No. 264 left for their base at Coltishall on 15th October and reequipped with the Meteor NF.11 (a night fighter based on the Meteor T.7) some twelve months later.

Aircraft servicing was 1st and 2nd line with four hangars available for use - the fifth hangar virtually destroyed in the August 1940 bombing was just a shell with the floor now used as a vehicle hardstanding. Major work required on the Meteors was carried out at RAF maintenance units but usually by civilian contractors at their aerodromes/factories. Further extensions to the concrete apron were started on 11th December 1950 when civil engineering contractors H. Boot & Son Ltd were recorded as having begun work on a refuelling apron.

Late in 1950 Pilot Cadets spent a few weeks at Driffield waiting to join a course at No. 2 Initial Training School RAF Digby in Lincolnshire and at this time were billeted in one of the Barrack Blocks. Little seems to have been arranged but the Station Flight Oxford was used on a variety of tasks around the local area often flown by the Flying Wing Adjutant. There were severe snowstorms in the Yorkshire area at the end of 1950 and Pilot Cadets spent days and nights clearing the runways and taxiways so that flying could recommence. A sudden thaw then occurred!

Announcements in January 1951 of RAF expansion plans and rearmament included the call-up of Reservists. The urgent demand for pilots brought further thoughts about the training programme not only with the opening of new basic flying schools but an expansion of the advanced schools. A reformed No. No. 202 AFS opened at Valley in Anglesey, North Wales on 1st April 1951 and the Vampire element of No. 203 AFS at Driffield left to join the new unit. Several fatal crashes involving the Vampire were recorded during the time they operated from Driffield. These were VF276 which crashed on take off at Driffield after losing a wing tank on 8th March 1950, VF308 and VF270 which collided near Driffield on 17th October 1950, VZ348 near Cottam having spun into the ground out of cloud on 27th October 1950, TG295 near Dishforth on 20th January 1951 and WA371 again near Cottam on 5th April.

A number of other jet training schools were formed to follow the example at Driffield from late 1950 through to early 1952. They were controlled by a new Group (No. 25), in Flying Training Command established for the purpose in March 1951 taking over administrative control from other groups in Flying Training Command during May 1951.

In February 1951, it was decide to evaluate the Vampire Two-Seat Trainer at No. 203 AFS - the prototype of this private venture was allocated the military serial WW456. It was delivered to Driffield on 8th March 1951 for an experimental training course and on 15th April after pilots had successfully completed the course, the aircraft was transferred to the Central Gunnery School at nearby Leconfield for further trials which were completed on 26th April.

Although the station had opened in 1936, approval to the use of a station badge was only given in April 1951 under a "block" system for a number of RAF stations by H.M. King George VI. The badge is described "In front of a York rose a shell". The station had included in its badge a shell, part of the crest of the Sykes family which had owned the land on which the airfield was situated.

Ray Hanna joined No. 24 Course and was at Driffield between 18th June and 4th September 1951, he had attained "wings" standard at No. 3 FTS Feltwell. He flew a number of different Meteors with instructors Flt Lt De Salis and later Flt Lt Carson, S/Ldr Ellis carried out checks on progress, most of the flying was carried out from Carnaby since the runway at Driffield was being repaired. Long range flights were part of the training bearing in mind the relatively short endurance of the Meteor. Visits were made to Little Rissington, Oakington, Valley, Hullavington and Finningley. The Meteors at this time had their nose caps painted either red or blue to denote the squadron within the school and continued to carry the "F" codes identifying the school as well as the individual aircraft. At the end of the course he passed out as an "above average pilot". One further duty at Driffield was as second pilot to fly from Carnaby to Feltwell and back in the station "hack" Oxford HN832.

Ray Hanna went on to further his training at No. 226 OCU Stradishall still flying the Meteor which he felt was a wonderful aircraft. In 1965 at the Central Flying School, he joined the Red Arrows Aerobatic Team as No. 3 in the formation under the leadership of Flt Lt L. Jones at the time the team had seven Folland Gnats. The following year as S/Ldr Hanna, he led the team then with nine Folland Gnats until 1969. He is still flying "warbirds" but with the Old Flying Machine Company at Duxford airfield giving considerable pleasure to a receptive audience.

Derek Scott was another National Serviceman who was posted to Driffield in June 1951. He had received his call up in November 1950, shortly after his 18th birthday and following a medical examination in Lincoln at the beginning of December went to Cardington in Bedfordshire for the usual formalities etc., including trade selection. Because of the possibility of going to Medical School after RAF service, he opted for the medical branch being "'talked" into signing as a 3-year Regular because the money was much better than ordinary National Service and the prospects also seemed much better. *He felt* " what the hell, an extra year wasn't going to make too much difference to *my life*".

Eight weeks recruit training was done at RAF West Kirby in the Wirral, but the station was a very cold place that winter. A posting to Moreton-in-Marsh, Glos, for trade training found that place was also very cold until well into spring. Instead of going home on leave after Moreton, Derek and five others went on a

No. 33 Squadron Venoms on the pan at Driffield.

(Phillip Rhodes)

A visitor to Burtonwood Armed Forces Day in May 1957 was this Venom NF 2A from No. 33Sqn.

(Barry Abraham)

Within a very short space of time, No. 219 got involved operationally with Exercise Beware which was held between 23rd September and 2nd October 1955. For the occasion, No. 92 Sqn from Linton-on-Ouse was attached using their North American Sabre F.4, altogether some 157 sorties were flown from Driffield by the two units. Participation in the exercise held up the conversion programme but No. 219 provided wing operations. The month of October continued with the conversion programme but since Driffield didn't have a Ground Controlled Approach radar, practice was carried out at Linton-on-Ouse and also the airfields at Strubby and Spilsby in Lincolnshire.

On 15th October No. 33 Squadron joined No. 219, having been reformed that day and also equipped with Venom NF. 2A. Most of the No. 33 Sqn Venoms had previously seen service with No. 23 Sqn at Coltishall in Norfolk which gave them up when reequipping with the NF.3 version. A similar establishment of Venoms, Meteors and a Vampire was allocated to No. 33. The Wing comprising the two squadrons was now complete, No. 219 occupied No. 4 Hangar and No. 33 used No. 1 Hangar by the public road.

The Venom, NF.2A was an improvement on the NF.2 and now had a clear canopy which helped night vision and better control due to modified fins and rudders. Only three RAF squadrons were equipped with the Venom NF.2A, the other one being No. 253 at Waterbeach in Cambridgeshire which actually outlived the Driffield squadrons since it was not disbanded until 31st August 1957. The Venoms had an interrupted pattern of dark sea grey and dark green on the upper surfaces with sea grey on the lower surfaces. Each squadron had its own special marking and method of identifying each aircraft in the unit. Both carried boom stripes, No. 219 a black rectangle with a red horizontal chevron and a red individual aircraft letter painted on a black background on the nose-wheel door. No. 33 had light blue, dark blue and red rectangles with individual letters inside the port flap as well as the nose-wheel door which had the letter in dark blue against a light blue background. Wing tip tanks were later painted with flashes, red for No. 219 and white and blue for No. 33. Venom WL862 was marked with the Group Captain pennant denoting Wing Leader.

Problems were experienced in operating the Venom NF.2A in that high altitude interceptions were difficult because of excessive cockpit icing. Poor weather also hampered training and Exercise Kingpin due to be held on 15th December was cancelled after a couple of hours after a Venom was scrambled but had to divert to Leuchars in Scotland because of bad weather. As 1956 opened concentration was given to weapon training over the Filey Bay range prior to Armament Practice Camp at Acklington. A Sector exercise took place on 12th January and many Canberra "kills" were claimed. The English Electric Canberra was the standard R.A.F. medium bomber of the day serving with No. 1 Group and No. 3 Group with more than twenty squadrons based at airfields in Lincolnshire, Norfolk and Cambridgeshire. The first of the "V" bombers, the Vickers Valiant was just entering squadron service and Finningley airfield near Doncaster was being rebuilt to house "V" bombers.

F/Lt Brian Murgatroyd joined No. 33 Sqn from No. 68 Sqn in Germany where he had been flying Meteor NF.11s. Most of the pilots for the new squadron had been drawn from the Meteor squadrons and none of them had flown Venoms. The Squadron Commander was Wg Cdr Patrick and Brian was allocated to "B" Flt under S/Ldr Ray Morley. "A" Flight was commanded by S/Ldr Caryl Gordon who earlier had taught the Duke of Edinburgh to fly at White Waltham, this connection gave rise to a "prank" during an official visit by the Duke of Edinburgh.

Brian Murgatroyd recalls "A typical day in the life of night fighter crews consisted of a met. briefing at about 0800hr and then the aircraft were flown in the morning on NFTs - Night Flying Tests to check the serviceability. Afternoons would be left for leisure or some general duty since every aircrew member held at least one other job such as Officer i/c Barrack Block, Orderly Officer or Operations Officer in the Control Tower.

After dusk, aircraft would take off in pairs to practice high speed and high altitude interceptions, initially under the control of ground radar, each crew taking it in turns to be target or attacking aircraft. Attacks were always head-on with ground control handing over to the Navigator/Radar Operator on the voice signal *Judy* and the pilot flew the interception pattern according to his radar operator's commentary.

Throughout the time we were at Driffield, both night fighter and day fighter squadrons operated on a rotation basis of full readiness, fully armed up, sitting in cockpits at the end of the runway, 24 hours a day and 365 days a year.

Team spirit was high and No. 33 Squadron had a "vehicle" for use as a hack, mainly to transport personnel to the local towns on recreation. It was a 1928 hearse painted red, white and blue with a dummy scanner on the roof denoting the all-weather search radar as used by the squadron. On the day of a visit by the Duke of Edinburgh, his chauffer and car were "stolen" and as a result, His Highness had to be conveyed around the station in the hearse, much to the amusement of everyone concerned! Later in the day His Highness was entertained at a "Dining In" night in the Officers' Mess.

One of the local hostelries used by the squadron was The Bell in Driffield and I was very interested to see on a recent visit, still proudly displayed on the Bar, the squadron plaque presented to them during the stay of No. 33 at Driffield.

Freezing conditions meant that the runway could not be safely used so the whole of No. 33 Squadron aircraft lined up, side by side, to direct the hot air gases from the single engines in an attempt to melt the ice, which they did but it was so cold, it promptly froze again."

The continuing bad weather prevented flying practice at the beginning of February but the departure of No. 219 to Armament Practice School at Acklington was achieved on the 6th. The squadron remained at Acklington until 9th March and air firing scores were good, one incident involved WL875 which overshot the runway following brake failure but no serious damage was caused to the crew or the aircraft. The Sector exercise later in March was not as successful as regards interceptions of the Canberra force.

The Group AOC AVM W.G. Cheshire carried out an inspection on 6th April which was accompanied by a fly past of Venoms and the same month a check was carried out by an inspecting team from the Fighter Weapons School at Leconfield (the Operations Record Book for No. 219 still records the school as being the Central Gunnery School!).

Venom WL848 of No. 219 unfortunately stalled in circuit at Driffield and crashed on 3rd May 1956 with two fatalities. The crew was F/O J.M.W. Galloway (Pilot) and Sgt Rice (Navigator). Three minor incidents affected No. 219's Venoms during the month, the starboard panel of the canopy of WL846 shattered during a fly past at Valley in Anglesey, North Wales. Then WL850 had to make a precautionary landing at Driffield due to brake pressure failure and the navigator in WL848 passed out at 43,000 ft but made a recovery upon descent.

Further exercises were carried out during June, July and August including one for the Royal Observer Corps which still had an aircraft reporting role in 1956. In August aircraft were sent to participate in the ROC Day at Church Fenton.

No. 238 OCU at Colerne in Wiltshire was tasked with training night fighter operators but also provided inspection crews to carry out standardisation flying with all wing navigators. Two Bristol Brigands and two Boulton Paul Balliols (which acted as the target aircraft) arrived on 24th July to perform this duty at Driffield. The Brigands and Balliols were piston driven aircraft and used at Colerne to train night fighter radar operators in locating and tracking hostile aircraft at night and in bad weather. The detachment was to check squadron radar operators and allowed the Squadron Navigator Radar Leader to fly with Navigator Radar personnel and advise any new techniques.

WL849 of No. 219 flying late at night on the 27th July in very heavy rain overshot the runway at Driffield which resulted in damage to the undercarriage and undersurfaces but the aircraft was repaired and returned to service.

No Battle of Britain display was held at Driffield in September 1956 but the squadrons did supply aircraft for other stations which were open to the public. For example, aircraft went to St Athan, Dishforth, Ouston and Aldergrove. This was the time when British and French forces were gathering in the Eastern Mediterranean following the nationalisation of the Suez Canal by Egypt. Driffield was host to No. 502 (County of Ulster) Sqn Royal Auxiliary Air Force operating Vampire FB.5 and FB.9s to give them flying practice devoted entirely to air firing. It appears that the "part timers" achieved very high scores on the flag through their attempt to show up the regulars! The annual Fighter Command exercise code name Stronghold dominated the end of September when 11 Canberras and one Meteor were claimed as destroyed plus an "Air France Stratocruiser" (aircraft recognition?) and a Lincoln bomber!

Venom WR785 of No. 33 hit a tree and High Tension cables after take off and crashed at Kirkburn 11/2 miles South West of Driffield during the night of 11th October 1956.

Detachments to Armament Practice Schools by operational squadrons was discontinued in November 1956 but in the case of Driffield a solid two weeks of air firing and exclusive use of a range was substituted. No.

About 1000ft to 1500ft away was the Launch Control Trailer and Missile Check-out Trailer. These were equipped with instrument panels and telephones for the Launch Control Officer (an RAF Flight Lieutenant) and US authentification officer (likely with the rank of Major) with a Launch Monitor Console Operator, three missile technicians and an electrical fitter/mechanic.

The actual missile site was also illuminated by floodlights mounted on pillars. Fire protection of the site was later provided by a central water tank which fed into an underground system of pipes to hydrants. Driffield also retained fire engines.

Phase I of firing the missile involved checks on the three pads whilst the missiles were lying horizontally in the shelter. Phase II, the crew would electronically roll back the missile shelter then using the powerful hydraulic launch erector lift the missile into the upright position. Phase III, once standing and temporarily se cured, the missile was fuelled. The remaining phases, i.e. firing would only take place if the missile was to be released and these only took place at the operational training base at Vandenberg in the United States. The entire sequence took about fifteen minutes and when the Launch Control Officer pressed the firing button, main engine ignited and burned for about 21/2 minutes. Ten minutes into flight it reached an altitude of 280 miles and at that point the re-entry vehicle containing the warhead, separated from the fuselage and began its descent down towards the target. Total flight time was about 18 minutes.

Driffield reopened in October 1958 within No. 1 Group, Bomber Command as Headquarters of the Driffield Wing and on the 3rd November 1958 the first USAF Military Air Transport Service aircraft landed at Driffield, five more came over the next few weeks. The USAF used C-124 Globemasters and C-133 Cargomasters to bring in all the equipment associated with the missile system. Altogether there were 76 flights into Driffield to complete the build-up by 1959. It is rumoured that one aircraft landed at Cottam by mistake and rapidly took off when this was realised. When Driffield airfield closed to aircraft operations, Leconfield was used with transport by road. The warhead was carried in a curtain sided trailer and the moves were in the greatest secrecy, a serviceman commented "it was like a wagon train with a convoy of heavily armed Americans, RAF Police and a Morris Commercial LD convoy fire engine".

Because Thor was a joint RAF/USAF programme there were a number of USAF Units and Detachments which had been assigned from the United States Strategic Air Command as part of the programme. From 1st January 1959 a detachment from the 672nd Technical Training Squadron, had been placed to help RAF personnel introduce this new weapon into service. It provided personnel for the maintenance and custody of the re-entry/warhead combinations and to provide launch authentication under Emergency War Order conditions. There was a USAF representative on duty at each Launch Control Station at all times that the squadron was capable of launch and weapon operations.

One of the American servicemen was Airman First Class Marvin Eugene Thomas whose son Steve has been able to provide some information for the period his father was based at Driffield between 1959 and 1961. A new facility to the RAF was two lane ten-pin bowling alley built at the south west end of the camp near to Hangar No.1 and Picture House converted from the Gymnasium building which is now used as the Rugby Club house.

RAF personnel had to be trained in the new technology and special introductory courses were arranged at RAF Flying College Manby in Lincolnshire between April and May 1959 although some academic training had been carried out at RAF Technical College Henlow in the previous year. The United States bore the cost of the missile and its development but the RAF carried the cost of the installation at the various bases which was estimated initially at ú1 3/4m when five squadron bases were envisaged. The training of 1000 officers and men for each complex was estimated at ú3.0m. During the build-up of the force, RAF personnel undertook training in the United States and the first firing by an RAF team was led by S/Ldr P. G. Coulson MBE DFC on 16th April 1959. Certificates of Training were awarded by the Douglas Aircraft Company Inc.

The first missiles arrived at Driffield on 3rd April 1959 with the last on 3rd November 1959, the airfield then closed and further flights were through Leconfield. Gp Capt R.T. Frogley CBE DFC assumed command in May 1959. Each of the new squadrons was formed on 1st August 1959. The Wing was organised with Wg Cdr W.A. Thynne O.C. Operations, Wg Cdr M.F. Hatton O.C. Technical Wing and later Wg Cdr F.C. Ellis as O.C. Administration Wing.

Each squadron in the wing essentially consisted of three Launch Emplacements, also referred to as pads, for Thor missiles.

155

No. 98 Sqn	Driffield	L/E	31/32/33	S/Ldr	P.G. Coulson MBE DFC
No. 226 Sqn	Catfoss	L/E	34/35/36	S/Ldr	E.R. Morriss
No. 150 Sqn	Carnaby	L/E	37/38/39	S/Ldr	E.R.G. Haines DFM
No. 240 Sqn	Breighton	L/E	40/41/42	S/Ldr	R.W. Steel
No. 102 Sqn	Full Sutton	L/E	43/44/45	S/Ldr	L.A. Baldchin

The Launch Emplacements were numbered in sequence from original installation and the missiles themselves carried individual identities being rotated between maintenance and also test firings in the United States. Thor missiles were easily identified since were not stored underground and consequently attracted the activities of the Campaign for Nuclear Disarmament. Thor operated on the same QRA (Quick Reaction Alert) basis as the "V" bombers.

Wing Headquarters at Driffield provided inspection and training needs of the various sites. RIM carried out periodic inspections of the missile pads after take over from Douglas but initially if snags occurred it could take a number of weeks to have them sorted. Squadron personnel went to Driffield for refresher training with the Field Training Detachment of the United States Air Force. Three days of theory then practical application, two days actual countdown training with a number of induced malfunctions. Driffield Categorisation Flight carried out checks on squadron sites. The Launch Control Officers courses lasted between three and five days on target insertion, use of short and long range theodolites and Control Electronics Assembly in the missile itself. Another course was the Propelled Transfer System held at Driffield.

Driffield also introduced a Continuation Training Syllabus in 1960, training for all personnel could be undertaken on a crew basis (became known as Flights) on their own sites. However, the USAF FTD gave Continuation Training Launch instruction at Driffield, representatives of Douglas and Rocketdyne tested individuals.

Frequent checks up to Phase III were carried out on site, one of the main risks involved was fuel catching fire. Several fires did occur with the result that fire fighting facilities were improved to minimise the risk of a serious fire breaking out and causing considerable damage. Regular practices were carried out to deal with fires. One of the great fears was a fire occurring. Most of the practice countdowns were "dry" to avoid accidents but Disaster Control Exercises were held - simulated fires on the Re-Entry Vehicle trailer, even radio reports had to be simulated! The Fire Section undertook specialist training including methods to avoid fire hoses becoming frozen during winter months. Wing Safety Officers and Bomber Command Fire Officers regularly visited all squadron sites as well as the Driffield Station Fire Officer.

The RAF Regiment was also called in to run "Passive Defence" courses at Driffield. Attendance by all personnel was mandatory. Following on to this was the Driffield Security Flight carrying out intruder exercises at the squadron sites.

These regular courses meant reorganising the shift system which caused some dislocation.

Three missiles of No. 98 (SM) Squadron were based at Driffield. The squadron had a nominal strength of 60 personnel - six officers, twenty nine SNCOs and twenty five other ranks which would give five six-man launch teams. In addition, there was the general administrative staff and RAF Police. The Launch Control Officer had a "shadow" being a USAF authentication officer. The U.S. forces had their own compound within the site in which the missile heads were stored and guarded by their own armed force. Shifts were worked 0800 to 1600, 1600 to 2400 and 2400 to 0800. Each shift being under the command of an RAF Flight Lieutenant.

No. 98 operated quite separately from the base headquarters being treated in just the same way as the dispersed squadrons with the exception that it had a double missile head storage building whereas the dispersed sites had a single building. Squadron commanders in the missile force tended to be the only member to be resident in the compound and living in an "L" shaped house but at Driffield because of the accommodation available on the camp, the commander lived in normal quarters. Wooden huts were erected for use as a guardroom and canteen.

Squadron headquarters were on the main station in a converted aircraft hangar which also had offices and an operations room later renamed Missile Control Centre. The list shown indicates the first commanding officers of each Missile Squadron, in succeeding years each was relieved by a new commanding officer. Squadrons were responsible to Wing Commander Operations rather than the Driffield Station Commander.

The initial carriage and handling trials of the four missile installation were made using dummies of representative shape and ballasted to give the correct weight and centre of gravity. The shape represented the Anti-Radar missile, the TV missile had a blunt nose.

Buccaneers were coming off the production line at a rate of two per month so the move required production flight testing and preparation for delivery to the Service to continue at Driffield. Eight production Buccaneers completed their flight testing and were delivered from Driffield in the period. These were XV350, XV351, XV353 to XV360.

For the staff of HSA operating at Driffield posed no problems, many had been away on trials with the Buccaneers at distant locations and for many this was as near to home as their normal working location. The conditions at Driffield were not quite as comfortable as base and the availability of stores items required telephone calls and transport or a trip into HOSM before going to Driffield, but it was for a limited period only.

A Piper Comanche G-ATNV owned by the Vertex Co. of Driffield had been based at Leconfield but increased activity there brought about a transfer to Driffield during 1967/68.

On 1st April 1977 the base was transferred to the Army and renamed Alamein Barracks. It was used as a section of The School of Mechanical Transport based on Normandy Barracks at Leconfield, also previously an RAF station.

The runways were removed and the control tower together with air raid shelters demolished. The Thor launching sites were still in existence up to the arrival of the Army when the airfield was converted to a cross country driving course and the sites were buried under mounds of earth. The remaining walls of No. 5 (Reserve) hangar, up to about the height of the windows, were demolished and the floor used as a vehicle park, the floor level door rails still exist. The four remaining hangars were converted to intervention grain stores. The hangar wall windows were replaced with louvres and two large ventilator ducts and the annexe windows permanently shuttered, the high level windows in the end doors were plated over on the external surfaces, but the openings can be seen on the inside.

The Army School of Mechanical Transport found that the facilities at Leconfield could not accommodate the numbers of students arriving for driver training, so the Driffield barrack blocks were used as overflow student billets The students were transported to and from Leconfield on a daily basis in civilian clothes and private hire coaches. As the facilities expanded at Normandy Barracks and on the change over to tri-service driver training the housing of students at Driffield ceased.

During this period of Army occupation the RAF used the MT yard and some of the buildings around it for vehicle operations and some of their unmarried personnel were billeted in the barrack block next to Station Headquarters. The married quarters on the south side of the A164 road housed Army and RAF families during this period.

A memorial to the memory of those killed in the air attack of the 15th of August 1940 stands at the camp main entrance in front of the ex-Station Headquarters building. Presented by the Driffield Branch of the R.A.F.A. on the 19th of August 1990 the memorial comprises a stone plinth together with a tablet bearing the coat of arms of RAF Driffield and the names of the six airmen, one WAAF, six soldiers and one civilian.

The RAF left Driffield for the last time on the 28th of June 1996 when the conclusion of a long association with the base ended at a ceremony attended by the C.O. of RAF Staxton Wold, S/Ldr. Nick Mullins, civic dignitaries, members of Driffield RAFA Branch, and ex-service men and women who had been based there. The RAF ensign was lowered for the last time and this together with a symbolic key was handed over by the RAF to the representative from the Defence Estates Organisation at Catterick. The Avro Lancaster from the Battle of Britain Memorial Flight made two fly-pasts of the camp.

In 2001 most of the camp presents a sorry sight, with the exception of a compound under the jurisdiction of the Army Cadet Corps. This compound encloses Station Headquarters, the Guard Room, Station Sick Quarters, Decontamination Centre & Mortuary and a Barrack Block. The area also includes the site of the Sergeants' Mess, destroyed in the August 1940 air raids, where a smallbore rifle range has been built. The buildings are all in general use and are in good order. The rest of the site from the Officers' Mess to the roadway behind the hangar line is fenced off, all the buildings in this area have their ground floor windows and doors boarded up and many have had the upper windows vandalised. The water tower and Decontamination Centre have been demolished together with the Watch Office and Control Tower. From accounts, demolition of the latter was more of a task than initially thought and eventually explosives had to be used. The grass areas have gone wild and the native wildlife has bred prolifically. The perimeter track remains, but is in poor condition away from the hangars, the runways, have disappeared and are reputed to have been used as hardcore for the Driffield by-pass, one Thor launch pad can be found, the bomb dump revetments are still visible but heavily overgrown.

The airfield is still under the control of the Army and used as a dry training area, the four "C" hangars are in good condition although modified for grain storage, and some are used as general storage warehouses. The remainder of the camp on the north side of the road is in the care of the MoD Defence Estates Organisation and is under the supervision of a security firm.

The Married Officers' Quarters to the north east along the road to Little Driffield have been sold off to private housing, the married quarters in Auchinlek Close, to the south of the main road, are in the control of the MoD Housing Executive and are being sold off. The wartime gymnasium, sometime camp cinema known to have been used on at least one occasion for the Royal Observer Corps Master Test aircraft recognition film, at Kelleythorpe was sold many years ago to the Driffield Rugby Union Club.

The memorial, previously mentioned, to those who lost their lives in the air raid in August 1940 is the only record existing on the site of the many who served on the airfield during its active life. A memorial subscribed to by the Nos 466 and 462 (RAAF) Squadron Association stands in the Remembrance Park in Driffield, crafted in Sydney, Australia, from dark grey granite, hewn from a quarry near Eugowra in mid-western New South Wales it honours the 482 men who gave their lives during the squadrons' service at Leconfield and Driffield during the period October 1942 to May 1945. This memorial was unveiled on the 12th of September 1993. In St. Mary's church, Beverley there is a Book of Remembrance for No. 466 (RAAF) Squadron. A plinth recording the sacrifice of members of Nos 102 and 405 (RCAF) Squadrons stands on the airfield at Pocklington near the Wolds Gliding Club, but this only records their time at Pocklington. A granite plinth within the area owned by the Yorkshire Air Museum, at Elvington records the time No. 77 Squadron served on that aerodrome. In the churchyard at Lissett there is a plaque set in limestone commemorating No. 158 Squadron's stay at that airfield.

During the 1939-1945 War the Driffield squadrons lost many aircraft and aircrew who failed to return from operations over Europe:

77 Squadron	Whitley III & V 13	Aircrew 42
102 Squadron	Whitley III & V 13	Aircrew 25
104 Squadron	Wellington II 16	Aircrew 84
405 Squadron (RCAF)	Wellington II 1	Aircrew 6
158 Squadron	Wellington II 12	Aircrew 62
1502 BAT Flight	Whitley V 1	Aircrew 3
466 Squadron (RAAF)	Halifax III 18	Aircrew 85
462 Squadron (RAAF)	Halifax III 7	Aircrew 20
	81 aircraft	327 airmen

In addition, 91 Aircrew were Prisoners of War until the war in Europe ended

The future of the main camp is not known at the time of writing, but one can only assume it will eventually find a buyer and then it is anybody's guess as to the future.

4 Gp TTF	2.40	Formed from Battle I Flt at Linton-on-Ouse	14.11.41	Redesignated 1484 TT Flt	Various Out based at Cottam 27.9.40 - 24.10.40 & 12.5.41 - 28.9.41 Amalgamated with 5 Gp TTF 29.12.40 - 2.4.42
5 Gp TTF	c. 14.2.40	Formed	29.12.40	Amalgamated with 4 Gp TTF	Various Revived with original designation and moved to Coningsby 2.4.41
97 Sqn	1.5.40	Reformed	20.5.40	Disbanded	No aircraft
88 Sqn	14.6.40	France	23.6.40	Sydenham	Battle I
2 (C) OTU dett	10.40	Catfoss	1941	Catfoss	
213 Sqn	15.1.41	Leconfield	18.2.41	Castletown	Hurricane I
1 Sqn RCAF	10.2.41	Castletown	1.3.41	Digby and renumbered 401 Sqn	Hurricane I
485 Sqn RNZAF	1.3.41	Formed	21.4.41	Leconfield	Spitfire I
5 SFTS dett	1.3.41	Ternhill	7.3.41	Ternhill (and later)	Master III
104 Sqn	1.4.41	Reformed	18.10.41	Air Echelon etc.	Wellington II
2 BATF	14.4.41	Linton-on-Ouse	10.41	Redesignated 1502 BATF	Whitley III, V Wellington I
405 Sqn RCAF	23.4.41	Formed	20.6.41	Pocklington	Wellington II
1502 BATF	10.41	Formed	23.7.43	Leconfield	Whitley III, V Wellington I
1484 Flt	14.11.41	Formed from 4 Gp TTF	1.4.42	Redesignated 1484 TT & G Flt	Battle, Lysander Whitley Various
158 Sqn	14.2.42	Reformed from UK echelon of 104 Sqn	4 - 6.6.42	East Moor	Wellington II
1484 TT & G Flt	1.4.42	Formed	18.12.42	Redesignated 1484 (Bombing) Gunner Flt	Defiant Martinet Various Affiliated to Air Bomber Training FLT 6.42 - 3.43
Air Bomber Training Flt (4 Gp)	17.6.42	Formed	15.3.43	Disbanded	Affiliated to 1484 (B) Gunnery Flt Oxford I

466 Sqn RAAF	15.10.42	Formed	27.12.42	Leconfield	Wellington II
196 Sqn	7.11.42	Formed	22.12.42	Leconfield	Wellington X
1484 (Bombing) Gunnery Flt	18.12.42	Formed from 1484 TT&G	23.7.43	Leconfield	Various
1613 AA Coop Flt	20.2.43	West Hartlepool	13.7.43	Hutton Cranswick	Henley Various
Air Fighting Dvt Unit dett (4 Gp) (Wittering)		Wittering	21.7.43	Leconfield	Various
6 AACU dett (Castle Bromwich)	6.43		13.7.43		Various
466 Sqn RAAF	3.6.44	Leconfield	8.9.45	Bassingbourn	Halifax III, VI To Transport Cd 5.45
462 Sqn RAAF	12.8.44	Reformed	29.12.44	Foulsham	Halifax III To 100 Gp Bomber Command 27.12.44
426 Sqn RCAF	25.5.45	Linton-on-Ouse	25.6.45	Tempsford	Ground crews only To Transport Cd 6.45
10 ANS	19/ 30.9.46	Swanton Morley	1.3.48	Disbanded into 1 ANS & 2 ANS	Wellington X Anson I
204 AFS	1.3.48	Cottesmore	15.8.49	Brize Norton	Mosquito III, VI 21 Gp
226 OCU	26.8.49	Bentwaters	31.8.49	Became 203 AFS	Vampire Meteor 21 Gp
203 AFS Based at Carnaby 7 - 9.50	1.9.49	Reformed from 226 OCU	1.6.54	Redesignated 8 FTS	Meteor F.4, T.7 Vampire FB.5 23 Gp to 21 Gp 1.5.51 RLG Carnaby 1.9.49 - 1.6.54
Aircrew Transit Unit	30.11.49	Digby	28.12.51	Cranwell	
264 Sqn	2.10.50	Church Fenton	15.10.50	Coltishall	Mosquito NF.30
8 FTS	1.6.54	Reformed from 203 AFS	22.8.55	Swinderby	Meteor F.4, T.7 Vampire (various) RLG Carnaby 1.6.54 - Full Sutton 21.7.54 - 1.6.55

BIBLIOGRAPHY

Action Stations No. 4 Yorkshire	B.B.Halpenny
Air Defence of Britain 1914 - 1918.	C.Cole & E.F.Cheesman
An Illustrated History of the New Zealand Spitfire Squadron	K.W.Wells
Armstrong Whitworth Aircraft Since 1913	O. Tapper
Balloons To Buccaneers	B. Catchpole
Bases of Air Strategy - Building of Airfields for the RAF	R. Higham
Battlebags	C. Mawthorpe
Bomber Command Losses (Series)	W.R. Chorley
Bomber Command War DiariesM.	Middlebrook & C. Everitt
Bomber Squadrons of the RAF	P. Moyes
Bombing Colours 1937 - 1973	M.J.F. Bowyer
Brave & True - the History of 466 and 462 (RAAF) Squadrons	S. Parker & A. Silverstone
Britain's Military Airfields 1939 - 1945	D.J. Smith
British Aviation - Ominous Skies 1935 - 39	H. Penrose
British Military Airfield Architecture	P. Francis
Control Towers	P. Francis
Countdown - Britain's Strategic Nuclear Force	AVM Stewart Menaul
Fighting Colours 1937-1975	M.J.F. Bowyer
From Hull, Hell and Halifax.	Blanchett
Handley Page Aircraft Since 1907	C.H. Barnes
In Brave Company. The Story of 158 (B) Sq.	W.R. Chorley
It's Suicide But its Fun -	P. Goss
My Airship Days.	G.F. Meager
Only Owls and Bloody Fools Fly at Night	Gp Capt Tom Sawyer DFC
RAF Nuclear Deterrent Forces	H. Wynn
R.A.F .Training & Support Units (Air-Britain)	R.C.Sturtivant et al
R.A.F. Squadrons.	Wg Cdr "Jeff" Jefford
Reap the Whirlwind.(6 Group RCAF)	Dunmore & Carter
Royal Air Force Serials (Air-Britain)	J.J. Halley
Royal Navy Aircraft Serials and Units 1911-1919 (Air-Britain)	R.C.Sturtivant et al
Squadron Profile No. 22 77 Squadron	C. Ward
Squadron Profile No. 34 102 (Ceylon) Sq	C. Ward
Squadrons of the RAF & Commonwealth (Air-Britain)	J.J.Halley
Strike Hard, Strike Sure. The Story of 104 (B) Sq.	R. Ginn
The Anson File (Air-Britain)	R.C. Sturtivant
The Royal Air Force - Illustrated History	Air Vice-Marshall M. Armitage
The Pendulum & The Scythe	K. Marshall
The Right of the Line	J. Terraine
The Royal Air Force Builds for War.	Published by The Stationery Office
The Unsinkable Aircraft Carrier	Duncan Campbell
The War in the Air Vols 1 - 6	Various
Twentieth Century Fortifications In England/ CBA Paper on Airfields	Dr. C. Dobinson
Twentieth Century Fortifications In England/ CBA Paper on Decoys	Dr. C. Dobinson

Vickers Armstrongs Wellington   K. Delve
Wellington - The Geodetic Giant   M. Bowman
White Rose Base   B. Rapier

OTHER SOURCES

Aeroplane Monthly March 1989 - The RAF's Thor Force   K. Delve
Airfield Review June 1985
Airfield Review April 1999 article - Emergency Runways   M. Osborn
Airfield Review July 1999 article - History of RAF Feltwell.   R.Towler & M.Osborn
Aviation News   21st March/3rd April 1975 issue   A. Pearcy
Correspondence from Wg Cdr Wally Dunn OBE to Colin Leadhill
      18.10.82, 26.8.83 and 13.1.84 of his time as Station
            Signals Officer at Driffield December 1939 to August 1940
Cross & Cockade International Journal Vol. 30 No. 2 (1999)
Driffield Post (newspaper)
Driffield Times & General Advertiser (newspaper)
Eastburn - the archaeology and history of an East Yorkshire Farm
      S. Harrison [Tom Lawton's memoirs used in Chapter 3]
Recruitment & Training (Royal Flying Corps) submission from
      H.R. Clarke (Cross & Cockade Society)
Squadron Newsletters of 77 Squadron and 102 Squadron Associations
The Aeroplane October 28, 1949   (Per Peter Berry)
To Defend & Deter - The legacy of the United States
      Cold War Missile Programme   J.C. Lonnquest and D.F. Winkler
RAF Flying Review   Vol XV No. 8